Death in the Northeast

DEATH in the NORTHEAST

NORTHEAST

by Josué de Castro

VINTAGE BOOKS
A Division of Random House
New York

The dead, never one of them here,
Come decked out in a coffin.
They are not buried,
But dumped into the ground.

Nenhum dos mortos daqui
vem vestido de caixão.
Portante èles não se enterram
São derramados no chão.—

João Cabral de Mello Neto in
Cemitérios Pernambucanos

PREFACE *to the Vintage Edition*

A country like Brazil—fifth largest in the world by territory and eighth by population—after a period of rapid economic development from 1930 to 1939, could fall abruptly into recession or, at least, economic stagnation. If analyzed objectively this could help us to understand the complex process of economic emancipation of developing countries, especially those in Latin America. Such understanding of the complexities that hinder the economic expansion in the regions with dependent economies has never been a matter of more urgency than now, when the countries of the Third World are experiencing their most serious historical crisis, watching the gap that separates them from rich and industrialized countries widen.

The political and social implications of the Brazilian

experience have a significance for the entire continent, and perhaps even more they offer an invaluable lesson for all who wish to think about development in economically backward areas.

We present here, therefore, a socio-economic analysis of one enormous region of a country as large as a continent, the region of Northeast Brazil, one of the most backward areas of the country and where, at the same time, out of truly appalling social conditions, rebellion has risen.

This book was written between October 1962 and February 1964. When a military coup ousted President João Goulart on the first of April, 1964, and established a new government in Brazil, the original manuscript was already in the hands of an English translator. The author's first impulse was to request its return to add a chapter dealing with the coup, linked as it is by impulse and political expression to the increasingly intense struggle in Brazil between the forces of national liberation and those that are holding back Brazil's socio-economic development. But, after careful consideration, the author decided to release the book as it had been conceived and written before the military coup of April 1, 1964. This decision was heavily influenced by his belief that he could not add anything that would clarify events better than the history of this explosive region and its sociological interpretation, as the author has tried to present it in this book, though at the time he couldn't know how or when the first explosions would occur. To add to it after the predictions were starting to come true would rob it of any significance as diagnosis and as a prognostication of the historical and cultural realities. It would be then a mere catalogue of the tragedies that Brazil is presently experiencing. The author has chosen, therefore, to publish the diagnosis as it was written before the fact.

The first edition of *Death in the Northeast* was published in the United States in 1966. Since it is now over four years since the military took over the government in order to, as they said, "save the country from the economic, political, and social chaos that threatened it," one might have hoped for some improvement in the situation in the Northeast. If such had been the case, if living conditions in that region had improved at all, then this document would no longer be pertinent. Unfortunately, this is not the case; there is no change and there is no improvement in conditions. The Northeast of Brazil remains a region of crisis where hunger and misery, instead of gradually subsiding, increase in intensity. Moreover, the tension there has become so threatening that a greater deployment of the forces of oppression is deemed necessary just to maintain order.

In the press we read frequently that even the Catholic Church (which has always been a conservative power) protests, through the authoritative voices of the bishops from the Northeast, against the inhuman condition in which the vast majority of the population of this region is kept. The Archbishop of Recife, Dom Helder Camara, never stops protesting the twin hungers, for food and freedom of the people of the Northeast. His public position, since he is a church representative who is identified with the people, has added to the political tension in the region. And the situation in the Northeast becomes more explosive at every moment.

Taking advantage of the financial help offered by SUDENE, an agency created several years ago to promote

the development of the Northeast, some industry was established in the area, which seemed to promise an improvement
in the living conditions and the possibility of some real
development in the countryside. Unfortunately, this was not
to be. The new industries sponsored by the SUDENE are
highly automated and are economically dependent on foreign capital or economic groups of the southern part of
Brazil. They cannot absorb the potential labor force that
exists in this region, any more than they can promote a more
equable distribution of wealth. The industrialization is
prototypically colonial; the wealthy class has been slightly
broadened, but the poor are stuck on the same level of
misery and despair.

The so-called "revolution" of 1964 had set as its chief
objectives an acceleration of the country's development
which had slowed in the years 1962-63, and as well a halt
to the inflationary process that had reached alarming levels.
To attain these objectives, the government of João Goulart
concentrated its efforts in promoting broad structural reform
that would liberate the production forces from the country's
archaic structures. The terror that these reforms inspired—
that they would inevitably end the privileges of the powerful
minority in favor of the long-suffering masses—eventually
brought the conservative military clique to the April, 1964,
coup. The fear of social revolution had dragged the country
to militarist counterrevolution.

The new military government was unable to bring about
the reforms that would have made it possible to meet even
its own stated goals. On the contrary, they had to prevent
that kind of reform; they were committed to preserving the
status quo. The government based its entire economic policy

on monetary control, without touching even slightly the basic structures that were holding back any true social and economic development.

The results of such an exclusively fiscal plan could only have been, as they were, disappointing. Neither was the inflationary wave held to the limit as they had forecast, nor did the economic impetus regain its desired speed. In its anti-inflationary policy the military government used two mechanisms that were greatly depressive: a violent drop of real wages and an excessive restriction of credit. This economic strategy tremendously impaired the situation of the working classes and threatened the very existence of the middle classes and of the small national industry that was being absorbed by the large foreign companies to which all kinds of favors were being extended.

An article published by *Time,* on December 6, 1966, states accurately that "the danger of de-nationalization of the Brazilian industry is not entirely imaginary." Quite truly, this danger is not imaginary, since this denationalization is taking place at ever-increasing speed, and is suffocating any real national industry. The national industry vegetates in economic stagnation, and in the total picture of accelerating underdevelopment those that must suffer most are the inhabitants of the Northeast, where the basic structures remain entirely untouched.

Since nothing has changed in the Northeast of Brazil, the author thought it unnecessary to alter the text of his book for a new edition, that he should keep it exactly as it had been written before the "revolution," whose premise was the preventing of any change in the socio-economic situation of this area. Its value as document in this way seemed more justified than a mere isolated statistical table that could have been updated. The author suggests that the interpretation presented in the book remains valid, and for this reason, he decided it should appear unchanged and unamended.

Paris, 1969   Josué de Castro

CONTENTS

Death in the Northeast

Il convient de noter d'abord que la science a un point de départ, que ce point de départ est donné par le sens commun.—Jean Wahl

(From the start it is useful to bear in mind that science has a point of departure and that this point of departure is given by common sense.)

Pensamos que a obra do sociológo será sempre una intervenção e que será enganar aos outros e iludir a si mesmo, se não tomamos em consideração esta verdade e a responsabilidade que ela comporta.—Camillo Pellizi

(We believe that a sociological work must always be in the nature of an intervention and that we shall only deceive both others and ourselves if we fail to take this truth, and the responsibility it implies, into consideration.)

INTRODUCTION

THE Portuguese discovered the Brazilian Northeast in 1500, the United States, in 1960, and both times it was by mistake—an error of navigation in 1500 and an error of interpretation in 1960. Much has been written about Pedro Alvares Cabral's accidental discovery, lost at sea while en route to the East. But almost nothing has been written about America's rediscovery five centuries later, when it was lost on sociology's figurative seas.

The present book proposes to document this second discovery and to make a modest contribution to the history of the rediscovery of the Brazilian Northeast in the light of a growing awareness outside, especially in the United States, of this troubled, long-suffering and socially explosive part of the world. I shall report the good and the bad, that which fills us with pride as Brazilians and that which makes us blush with shame. This book will be an updating of the famous letter of 1500,[1] written by Pero Vaz de Caminha, a clerk with the fleet of Cabral, to the king of Portugal, describing the marvels of the New World.

This will not be a neutral interpretation, a cold and rigorous analysis of the realities of the Brazilian Northeast. *Death in the Northeast* is a sociological study by one who is committed [2] to a partisan and progressive point of view. I deplore things as they are, and my deepest desire is to see them changed and improved. The last thing I would wish would be to cover up revelations which might be considered damaging to the ruling class. In my view, society must be understood as a developing process, not as a set piece. I do not expect, nor would I wish, the social process to hold still while I photograph it.

A great deal of sociological interpretation of Brazil as a whole, and the Northeast as its most problematic segment, has tended to be utopian in tone and static in concept in order not to be judged offensive to the existing power structure or because of an unconscious identification with this structure. Of course, all observation, even the most scientifically refined, is limited to the observer's experience. All scientific truth is relative and statistical, we are told, and this certainly holds true for the para-scientific truths of sociology. But imagine how great the distortions become when the observer, over and beyond these inherent limitations, shrinks from dealing honestly and objectively with anything that might disturb the status quo! A progressive sociology at least minimizes this defect. It dares, even seeks, to confront the most difficult, disturbing aspects, as it must if

it is to help the people, its subject, escape the morass of poverty and social deprivation.

Moreover, the fact that I am a son of the Northeast, familiar from childhood with its problems and its psychology, though it cannot help but make me a regionalist in point of view, does also bring me close to the deepest feelings of the people and allows me to describe them with authority. The outsider could not know the people of the Northeast, the idiomatic quality of their life, as well as one who springs from their midst. Therefore, what I may lose in scientific extension and breadth, I gain in intention and depth. I view the social realities of Northeast Brazil *sui generis,* rather than as a corollary to some universal theorem. I am aware also that social unrest in the Northeast has its analogues in underdeveloped and exploited regions all over the world. But the specifics of its situation concern me more than the generalities, and with this in mind I have not hesitated, when the need has arisen, to move out of sociology into geography, economics, anthropology, ethnography and other disciplines.

My thesis is simple, though its subject—the people of the Northeast—is not. I believe that the twenty-three million inhabitants of this unfortunate region are rapidly gaining a political consciousness and a human identity. They are in a state of turbulent emergence. The Northeast of Brazil has as great an explosive potential as the Congo, South Africa, India or Vietnam. Though the suppressed masses have not yet been exposed to the propaganda and revolutionary leadership that exist in many other nations in a similar stage of emergence, explosive potential is not lacking. It is waiting for someone to light the fuse.

What I want to do, for the sake of the forgotten millions not only of the Brazilian Northeast but also of the rest of the world, is to present a clear idea both of the extent of the struggle for emancipation in this remote part of the world, and of its ineluctable necessity. Adverse historical circumstance and the errors and omissions of both national and international politics obstruct this struggle, so that the people must hew their way forward as through a thicket. Yet forward they come, little by little, step by step. Let us look at them as they strain. And beware.

chapter 1

SIX FEET UNDER AND A COFFIN

J oão Firmino, an employee of the Engenho Gal-
iléia, or the Galilee Sugar Mill, founded the first Peasant
League in the Brazilian Northeast in 1955. What Firmino
intended was not primarily, as one would think, the improvement of living conditions in the sugar-growing region.
He was not rising to the defense of the people of the countryside—these sad half humans crushed like cane between
rollers that leave only juiceless husks behind. Actually, the
Leagues' original purpose was to advance the interests of
the dead, victims of hunger, misery and the degradations of
the *bagaceira*, as Brazilians of the sugar mills call the sheds
where the cane residue, or bagasse, is stored. Firmino's aim

was to secure for the peasants the right to six feet of earth in which they might rest their bones, and beyond this, the privilege of being buried in wooden coffins of their own.

Fair play for the dead was the Peasant Leagues' initial objective; death was the first concern, since life had so little promise. But what provoked this obstinate insistence on six feet of earth in the other world by people who had never owned a single inch in this one? Why should these landless, disinherited masses harbor a desperate yearning to be buried in a coffin of their own, when in life neither land nor house had been theirs? Nor even, for that matter, had their own bodies and souls, since they had always been under lease to the lords of the land. Why this sudden departure from the usual apathy and resignation of the Brazilian peasant?

None of this makes sense until we understand that for the farm and plantation worker of the Northeast it is death, not life, that really counts. From life he gets nothing but suffering and backbreaking toil—under the constant threat of drought, hunger and disease, while the police lurk forever in the wings. Death alone is certain, safe and guaranteed. It is the one right no one can take from him.

It is this circumstance that accounts for the peasants' interest in the ceremonials that surround death. In the Northeast dying is looked upon as a liberation from life's endless oppressions. "Blessed are the poor," the Scriptures say, "for theirs is the Kingdom of Heaven." It is to this promise that the people turn for consolation, having lost all hope of succor in the earthly kingdom.

At the time the first Leagues came into existence (after more than four centuries of a feudal agrarian regime im-

planted by Portuguese colonists in the form of sugar plantations worked by slave labor[1]—a regime which was implac-
ably resistant to any amelioration of the living conditions)
the peasants were convinced that their plight was all but
sealed. The popular ballads of the Nordeste recount the he-
roics and the promise of peasant revolts in the past. They
tell about the *Balaiada,* an uprising in Maranhão,
1838–40. For reasons that are now obscure, one of the
leaders of the revolt, Manuel dos Anjos Ferreira, was pe-
joratively called *O Balaio* (a straw basket or small
hamper) and his followers were nicknamed *Balaios.* They
also tell about the Republic of Palmares, 1630–97, which
was set up in the backlands by runaway slaves under the
leadership of the famous Zumbi. They recall, as well, the
great rebellion in 1897 in the Northeast interior, led by a
fanatic religious leader, Antonio Conselheiro, from his
headquarters in the little village of Canudos. The folk singers at fairs have always extolled the indomitable courage of
the people's leaders who gave their lives for justice. Yet all
these things happened long ago and the peasants know very
well that their efforts and the resort to violence actually accomplished very little.

Brazil's Negro slaves, originally brought from Africa
by the Portuguese colonists, were freed in 1888. But were
they really emancipated or merely freed from the name of
slave? The fact is that whether he was slave or serf, farm-
hand, sharecropper or leaseholder, the Brazilian peasant,
at least in the Northeast, has always been accustomed to
forced labor, hunger and misery. The legacy of slavery remains in force, and will, as long as the Brazilian latifundian system of great landholdings prevails.

For four centuries this same latifundian system provided political consistency and an economic base for a developing country. Thanks to the great land grants by the Crown in the sixteenth century, Portugal gained a monopoly on sugar in the European market. But this was done by enslaving both men and the earth—by placing them unconditionally at the service of the feudal barons who wanted to get rich quick by producing more and more sugar. Meanwhile, the planters, blind to its consequences, gave themselves over with supreme dedication to their sugar venture and let no sentiment stand in their way. Nothing mattered but the golden juice of the cane; new lands to be swallowed up by the cane fields, more backs to be broken, year upon year, planting and harvesting the cane, hauling the cane carts along the roads, feeding the crushers at the mills, loading the sacks of raw sugar at the docks.

In some respects the physical appearance of the sugar country of the Northeast has changed with time. Great modern extraction plants have replaced the old-fashioned sugar mills powered by steam or water, which in turn had replaced the oxen. Today the "big house" of other years with its slave quarters attached has been replaced by a splendid villa. But the human landscape remains virtually the same. The former slaves, who once lived in the *senzala* near the big house, are now scattered in huts and shacks, lost in the fields or huddled in villages, or rotting in city slums. These are the new slave pens, and they are hardly better than the old. The latifundian system remains in effect unbroken.

Indeed, thus far the violence has served no useful purpose. Neither the bullets of the *cangaceiros*, as the bandit gangs of the Northeast backlands were known, nor the zeal of the mystics has been able to put an end to the peasants' dumb suffering and servitude. Nothing was accomplished by Antônio Silvino or Lampião, bandit heroes of folklore. Father Cícero of Joazeiro and his mystic cult did not in any way release the people from their fate. Like the cane carts, the people's destiny has been mired for centuries in the soft clay of the cane-field roads, stuck fast in the yielding and viscous *massapê*, the famous and endlessly fecund black soil of the Northeast coastal strip. The harder they have tugged and strained to free themselves, the more the great cart of fate has stuck fast, as if the devil himself had it by the wheels.

Actually, a whole constellation of factors have combined to produce a situation in which the hungry cannot eat because they cannot produce, and cannot produce because they cannot eat. But the man of the backlands knows little of these larger matters, only the immediate reality of his stagnation and entrapment. He looks on mutely as the rich grow richer at his expense. And in his frustration he shrugs his thin shoulders and says: "That's how it is in this world, water flows only to the sea, and money to those who have it." Often this inexorable flow leaves the dry earth of the backlands in extremity. At such a time the rural people of the Northeast may as a final resort harden their hearts and turn to banditry.

Again and again a feeling of total impotence and worthlessness has possessed the soul of the Northeasterner. From this has come his attitude of absolute humility and resignation in the face of what he too frequently sees as an ineluctable conspiracy of natural and social forces that combine to crush even a pretense of bettering his living conditions.

Thus the humble country folk of the Galilee Sugar Mill founded the Peasant League movement, not to demand their political rights, to advance Communist theory or to fight against exploitation, but merely to make a good show one day in the eyes of God by having a decent burial. Even on this small point their aspirations seemed excessive to the landowners, their fellow Christians.

It must be understood that traditionally in the Nordeste a poverty-ridden peasant is taken to the cemetery in a "charity" coffin lent by the government. But this coffin proceeds no farther than the mouth of the grave. The body is removed and buried, and the coffin is returned to serve other cadavers. This travesty of a ceremony was the supreme humiliation, a mortification that seemed to the peasant to carry over even into eternity. The first League was created to escape this shaming.

When he was interviewed by a newspaperman in 1960, one of the principal League leaders, old José Francisco de Souza, in answering a query about what the League had done for the peasants, calmly said: "Young man, before the League, when one of us died, the coffin was just lent by the government; and after the body had been carried to the common grave, the coffin went back to the municipal warehouse. Today the League pays for the funeral, and the coffin is buried with the dead. That's what the League did for us, my boy."

This was the first tangible result of the initiative by João Firmino and his fellow workers of the Galilee Sugar Mill. At first they called their new organization the "Farming and Stock-Raising Society of the Planters of Pernambuco." But soon they were calling it simply the "League," which its detractors turned into the "Peasant League." The pejorative title was intended to suggest guilt by association, implying that the League had hidden ties with the revolutionary peasant movement begun in other parts of the Northeast many years before—a movement which sought to unite the cane workers and give them enough political power to promote better living and working conditions. These earlier organizations had been called Peasant Leagues, probably under the remote inspiration of the Peasant Leagues of the Middle Ages, which European serfs had formed against feudal oppressors. In this general connection it must be remembered that Brazilian colonization in the Northeast sprang straight out of a feudalistic, medieval background. The Crown undertook to colonize Brazil through a system of enormous land grants to the Portuguese nobility. These land grants, called captaincies or fiefs, were originally roughly fifteen in number; each grant extended fifty leagues (about two hundred miles) along the coast and indefinitely inland. The grantees took the name of *donatários*. They had the power to found cities, levy taxes and subdivide their holdings. The Crown reserved the right to impose export taxes and to have a monopoly on exports of Brazilian spices and dyewood. Only ten of these fiefs were ever actually occupied by their owners, and only two proved viable. When the captaincy system proved inefficient, the *donatários* were stripped of their political power but allowed to keep the land. In time the captaincies were divided into *sesmarias*, or vast plantation holdings, still within the feudal tradition of the inalienable ownership and arbitrary use of the land by a tiny privileged minority who had aristocratic connections. Meanwhile, growing sugar cane had rapidly replaced cutting dyewood as the principal enterprise; this led to the introduction of a large number of Negro slaves from West Africa to work the plantations, which reinforced the archaic feudal arrangement to such degree that it persists in Northeast Brazil to this day.

At the beginning of the sixteenth century, when Brazil was being colonized, most of Europe was experiencing the full tide of the Renaissance. However, the two countries of the Iberian Peninsula, Spain and Portugal—preoccupied by an endless struggle with Islam and geographically isolated behind the Pyrenees—remained stuck fast in agrarian feudalism.[2] Of the two, Portugal was the more insulated, since it was cut off by a second mountain barrier that surrounded the Castilian tableland. Because of this lag in the homelands, both Spanish and Portuguese colonization in the New World was medieval in character (a hangover from the Crusades) and permeated with a spirit both religious and warlike, mystical and at the same time motivated by unbridled greed. In sum, the Iberian thrust westward bore little resemblance to the English type of colonization in North America, which was bourgeois and modern in spirit and completely Protestant in its psychology.

The Portuguese colonists brought over with them a feudal way of life, the serf-master relationships of the great seignorial estates of Portugal. Under different circumstances this medieval baggage could well have included the Peasant League tradition (found all over Europe in late medieval times among the peasantry) of collective resistance to the rigors of living in hereditary bondage with little or no chance of ever owning one's own plot of land. Such Leagues had often risen in bloody revolt. And in the Brazilian Northeast they were to do the same when the pressure grew intolerable. This was the case with the first League, of the Galilee Sugar Plantation. It is noteworthy that after electing their first "board of directors," the peasants, in a traditional gesture of humility, invited the plantation owner himself to be their honorary president.

The great man accepted their offer and solemnly took office with festivities and fireworks, while his honorific supremacy was duly incorporated into the new society's constitution. Encouraged by the apparently favorable reception, the peasants also wrote into the constitution such distant objectives as the acquisition of seeds and farm tools and possibly small-scale government subsidies. But these were merely tentative goals; funeral benefits were the immediate purpose.

The honeymoon at Galilee did not last long. Nearby planters hastened to warn the Galilee landlord that he was mad to get involved in such a perilous venture. Did he not see that he was allowing weeds of social agitation to run riot on his land? The Peasant League was a Trojan horse, ready-made to smuggle in Communist intruders. The planter took fright, resigned his presidency and demanded that the League be abolished at once.

Most of the peasants resisted. From this time on, under the pressure of events, what had started off as a mutual-death-benefits group became a full-blown political movement to secure peasant rights and freedom from landlordism. The defense of the dead became the defense of the living.

The story goes that the plantation owner got back at his workers for refusing to give up their League by canceling an order that permitted them to cut wood on his land in order to build a chapel. When the peasants protested, the *patrão* threatened police action, claiming that they would be damaging his woodlands. In due course came court warrants, summonses to the police station and finally threats from the *capangas*, the planter's hired gunmen.

This only hardened the peasants' hostility. Next their leaders were brought to court and accused of agitation and terrorism. This led to wholesale eviction; peasants were summarily kicked off land where they had lived all their lives. At this point they began to fight back in earnest, refusing to leave peacefully like so many sheep.

The fact is, no people in the world are more deeply rooted to the earth than the peasants of Northeast Brazil. In this way they are like the Chinese, who have suffered periodic cataclysms for thousands of years and still hold fast to the land. The German philosopher Hermann Keyserling[3] once wrote of the Chinese peasant: "No other peasant in the world gives such an impression of total identification with the earth, of participating so intensely in the life of the soil. Everything in China, all life and all death, unfolds in the hereditary earth. Here man belongs to the earth, not the earth to man." This description is equally true of the people of the Nordeste, the *camponês* of Northeast Brazil. But they are not known as well.

The Northeast is an isolated region, and the people who live there have always been virtually abandoned by the rest of Brazil and the rest of the world. The peasant has reacted to his isolation by clinging all the harder to the land. Even the inhabitants of the *sertão*, the dry hinterland of the Northeast, who are dispersed time and time again by fierce

dry spells that shrivel the land, always desire to return once
the drought has passed. Peasant names in the Northeast
have an earthy flavor, since they are derived from the villages or localities where their owners are born. Some typical names are: Antônio Pedro Joazeiro—Joazeiro is a town
in Bahia; Juca da Serra Talhada—Juca from the "Cut
Mountains"; and Manoel João de Lagoa Grande—Manoel
João from the "Big Lake." Like medieval names, these sur-
names, as the backlands writer Luiz da Câmara Cascudo
remarks with a certain pride,[4] link man to the earth.
Though he has known nothing but suffering from it, the man
of the Northeast defends his tie to the land to his last
breath.

Nevertheless, legal measures were taken to expel the
peasants of the Galilee Sugar Mill from their ancestral
homes. Because they were ignorant, they needed legal
counsel to fight back. But lawyers cost money and the
League cashbox was almost empty. In this crisis the League
officers turned to an obscure attorney who had defended
other peasants in eviction suits. The lawyer's name was
Francisco Julião.

Julião began a legal struggle to keep the peasants from
being driven out of Galilee. But he soon discovered that the
civil code, designed to ensure the dominion of the rich, was
of little value in defending the interests of the poor. The
only law at the peasants' disposal was the penal code.[5]
Thus, with the law proven useless, Julião turned to politics
and was elected a deputy to the Pernambuco State Assem-
bly.

In this way Francisco Julião the lawyer gradually
turned into Julião the agitator, the people's spokesman in

denouncing the crimes of the plantation system. The Peasant Leagues began to spread throughout the Northeast. New centers were formed to promote political action, and the Leagues began to develop an ideology, to proselytize and indoctrinate. In response, landlordism became even more violent and oppressive, and by 1957 or so the battle was truly joined.

Now that the struggle was out in the open, the newspapers began to take note of the more important skirmishes. The peasant cause found short shrift in the press, which described League activities as being led by "terrorists" and ran the accounts on the police page. Soon, however, the subject was considered important enough to be moved up to the political pages, and it became a matter of endless editorial comment. As the Leagues grew in stature and acquired political momentum they began seriously to frighten the ruling class of the Nordeste. The League was portrayed as an evil dragon intent on swallowing up the feudal estates and destroying public order and tranquillity and the whole wealthy establishment. A cloud of confusion and inaccurate reporting hung over the gathering conflict. As the Leagues grew, both sides retreated into extreme positions. Solid citizens began to speak of the League movement as if it were the Apocalypse. Julião was labeled an Antichrist.

It was at this juncture, about 1960, that the United States began to wake up to the situation in the Brazilian Northeast, in great measure because of the activities of the *Ligas Camponesas*. The United States, alerted by Fidel Castro's Communist revolution in Cuba, became extremely sensitive to the possibility that Communism might spread to all of South America. When the Peasant Leagues began to make headlines in Brazil, the American press started to pay close attention to the possibility of an imminent explosion. Americans had become vaguely familiar with the Northeast during World War II, when Natal had for a time the biggest airport in the world and was a main stopover on transport flights to and from Africa and Europe. Now, when it appeared that another Castro might be emerging in terra incognita, the Northeast experienced a kind of rediscovery.

Like Cuba, the Brazilian Northeast, at least in the coastal area, was dominated by large estates, frequently absentee-owned, and given over to a one-crop sugar-cane agriculture. Like Cuba too, the Northeast was both steeped in misery and seething with rebellion. Again like Cuba, the Northeast was the scene of an incipient revolt led by a man, Francisco Julião, who was considered a Marxist. Julião was leading disinherited masses toward revolution, and under his spell they seemed fanatically ready for anything. This theme was developed in major American newspapers and was documented starkly in a TV film report by one of the large American networks. Rapidly an image took shape: the Brazilian Northeast, as reported in the United States, was another oppressed region on the verge of a Communist-led revolt—another foreign situation of great gravity with which the United States had to reckon.

The result is that now the Northeast is at least a little in the public eye. It must be said, however, that the presentation of its discontents has largely distorted both the past, which generated them, and the programs aimed at relieving them. Both the possibilities and the defects and difficulties of the Northeast have been misrepresented. As for the role of the Northeast in peace and security, this too has been misconstrued. The American press has not correctly assessed the potential, good or bad, of this troubled and long-suffering region.

Thus the Northeast, which was discovered once when it aided the United States in the last war and was now rediscovered when it seemed to be aiding the enemies of the United States on the continent, continued to be in fact unknown to the United States and the whole world.

This first chapter has concentrated on the Peasant Leagues, with the deliberate intention of showing how an enterprise which sprang straight from agrarian feudalism —a movement with peaceful and humanitarian objectives —can be transformed into a revolutionary instrument by blind incomprehension and recalcitrance of the ruling class. However, the picture of the Peasant Leagues as a tool of international Communism, planned in Moscow and introduced into the Brazilian Northeast in an attempt to repeat Cuban triumphs and proceed from there to Communize the whole continent, is totally false. This cliché invented by the Western press does not stand up under a frank analysis.

It is closer to the facts to see the Peasant Leagues as motivated by a primitive Christian spirit that still permeates the collective soul of the Northeast. The fact is that during one phase of their development the Leagues were regarded with suspicion by Marxist leaders of the region, who tenaciously opposed them. If the Leagues later joined with the Communists in a common struggle toward emancipation of the rural masses, it does not mean that their inspiration derives from Marx or from Castro. The Leagues arose spontaneously from the peasant mass, a natural consequence of the unequal struggle to realize minimum aspirations against maximum resistance on the part of feudal oppressors. The American reporter Robert Coughlan,[6] writing in *Life* magazine, is correct when he says that to attribute social discontent in Latin America "to a Moscow-inspired plot, as many do, is to be dangerously ingenuous. Its roots run deep into the past, and include conquest, exploitation, hunger and extreme misery."

In any event, the Peasant Leagues did bring the Northeast to life in the American press and were one of the many factors that led to the creation of the Alliance for Progress, the American plan that was to thwart a presumptive bolshevization of Latin America. But it is my opinion that the Peasant Leagues never achieved any definitive political importance. They never achieved a firmness of structure and vigor of leadership to the point where they could unleash true revolution; as a revolutionary instrument, they have been little more than a child's toy. It is an index of the magnitude of the feudal landlords' guilt and fear that a mere toy should frighten them nearly out of their wits. These heartless people have reached a stage where they are choked with terror by the least reaction of the plundered masses. They see the least move toward justice as the end of their ancient privileges. But in cold fact the peril represented by these pathetically romantic Peasant Leagues has always been small, while fear of them is disproportionately great and grows daily greater.

chapter 2

600,000 SQUARE MILES OF SUFFERING

THE face of the Northeast is deeply marked by suffering. For centuries both man and earth have been martyred by adverse forces—natural and cultural. The marks of suffering are so much in evidence that one has the impression the whole landscape of the Northeast is a 600,000-square-mile stage set for some high tragedy.

The Brazilian Northeast runs from the state of Alagôas in the east to the state of Maranhão in the west. It is made up of a number of different climates, types of soil, kinds of vegetation and socio-economic organizations. But for our purposes we may divide the region into two parts: the eastern, coastal area and the western interior—the coastal re-

gion of the sugar plantations, and the drought region of the
hinterland, or *sertão*. The growing of sugar has always
shaped life in the coastal Northeast; and periodic drought
has been the main factor conditioning life in the backlands.

Climatically the two Northeasts are quite unlike. The
coastal region gets plenty of rain, but rain is scarce in the
interior and the whole region has a semiarid look. The two
landscapes are in sharp contrast. One has a green carpet of
endless cane fields that replaced the green of the forest. The
other is dominated by tones of gray; the dry earth, if not
exactly naked, is dotted with clumps of low vegetation covered with dust and bristling with spines. Here xerophytic
plants, such as the bromeliads and cactuses, abound. The
coastal strip has deep, porous, permeable, rain-soaked soil,
the famous *massapê*, highly fertile and ideal for growing
sugar cane. The soil in the interior is poor and sandy and
baked hard by the sun. Within these two natural frames two
societies have developed, distinct but complementary. The
socio-economic experiences of these two neighboring communities make up the historical patrimony of the Northeast.

Although this region has accumulated through the years
a great store of tradition and an appreciable, unique cultural wealth, its greatest fruit has been suffering; the principal legacy of the Northeast is the wretchedness that has
been handed down from generation to generation. And no
land gives a stronger impression of suffering than the
sertão, with its skin baked and corroded by the rigors of the
climate. The sandstone cover is so heavily eroded and de-
nuded that in places crystalline rock shows through the
granitic surface, and the soil is a thin and meager layer,

with outcroppings of jagged rock protruding like bare bones. There is a deep poignancy, an air of desolate suffering, in this wounded land, its sides riven by flash floods.

Another feature of the ravaged landscape that arrests the eye and oppresses the spirit is the dryness of the earth. In certain seasons the land lies scorched and cracked like an old piece of leather that has been left too long in the sun. Some of these parched areas in the backlands are tracts that were exhausted in a few years by sugar-cane monoculture, which insatiably devours the humus of the soil. I intend to analyze the history of this self-consuming sugar-cane culture in greater detail later on. It is the main feature of the great speculative adventure that produced the society of Northeast Brazil.

Against the background of this land, betrayed by its climate, stricken by drought and degraded by a plantation monoculture, the relentless suffering of the people stands out. Man's dying rather than his living stands out most prominently in the Northeast. Death is such a pervasive presence that in some towns in the interior the cemetery is the most attractive spot in the community. Walled, cultivated and carefully tended, cemeteries are the only verdant corners in towns that otherwise are apt to be a maze of sordid alleys, lacking any semblance of order, common hygiene and human comfort. A poet of the Northeast, contemplating these cemeteries, was troubled by the walls that separated them from human habitation, since on both sides there was a closeness to death.

Why all these walls?
Why isolate the tombs

From the more general boneyard,
The defunct countryside? *

The mortality rate in the backlands, particularly for infants, is among the world's highest. So many children die that sometimes it seems that more people must be dying than are born to live on. This illusion stems partly from the fact that whereas birth is a private affair, death always demands an ostentatious public funeral. As in Sicily, China and other places where people are closely tied to the land, a great point is made of man's return to the earth. And a vast number return very early, within months after birth. As a matter of fact, in some parts of the Northeast the mortality rate of infants actually exceeds 50 per cent, and more children are born to populate heaven with angels, as their parents imagine, than to populate the earth. Characteristic of such areas as the Brazilian Northeast is the cruel geography of hunger, a strange geography where the earth does not feed man so much as man the earth. And those who escape this inversion are always only a step ahead of Death, which breathes down their necks.

What is the reason for this pitiless mortality? The Northeast is an underdeveloped area, and underdevelopment always generates both high birth and high death rates. In both instances the figure for the Northeast is the highest in Brazil. In spite of a shockingly high mortality rate, the population tends to increase explosively, and as misery piles up, the stage is set for rebellion.

* *Por que todo êste muro?*
Por que isolar estas tumbas
Do outro ossário mais geral
Que é a paisagem defunta? 1

Some see this high rate of reproduction as a biological assurance of the survival of the species: an expendable majority are sacrificed, but enough are left to guarantee the continuance of the species. Actually, the situation is not so simple. A whole complex of interrelated biological and social factors accounts for the seeming paradox of concurrent high birth and death rates. I have attempted to explain the phenomenon in *Geography of Hunger*, and it is not necessary to repeat the same arguments here. For our purposes the hard statistical fact will suffice. As the people say: "The poor man's table is bare, but his bed is fertile." Fornication is the poor man's pleasure.

What causes so much dying in the Northeast? People die of everything, of course, but mainly they die of hunger —hunger in multiple disguises is the most active of the four horsemen. Hunger kills as a disease—the most serious and generalized of the mass diseases of underdeveloped regions—and also by making way for other sicknesses. These secondary killers are principally infectious bacilli and parasitic organisms, which flourish in these areas.

Nor is it a single type of hunger that decimates the population. In the coastal sugar area we find a chronic, endemic type of hunger, whereas in the backlands there are epidemics of starvation which occur in periods of drought. But to understand how these two kinds of hunger have come to reign in the Northeast, we must consider closely the socioeconomic structure.

When the nutritional conditions of the sugarland are examined, one is immediately struck by the sharp contrast between agricultural potential and an extreme shortage of edible crops. It is easy to explain why the arid wastes of the

Sahara or the impenetrable forests of the Amazon should be starvation areas. In these places hunger is predicated on the natural environment. But hunger in the sugar-growing section of the Northeast cannot be explained by natural causes, and it is all the more shocking on that account. The soil here is mostly *massapê*—a rich, black, clayey soil which lies in a thick porous mantle over the Cretaceous clayey shales and calcareous rock. *Massapê* is wonderfully fertile, rich in humus and mineral salts. The climate, with predictable rainy seasons but spared the excessive moisture of other tropical regions, would also make for the easy and dependable cultivation of a great variety of cereals, fruits and vegetables. The original forest contained an exceptional abundance of trees bearing edible fruit, while other fruit trees, transplanted from distant places, were soon as much at home in the Northeast as in their original habitat. The breadfruit, the coconut, mango and jack tree, the last a cousin of the breadfruit—all brought in by the Portuguese colonizers from the Far East—adapted well and produced exceptionally valuable food. Everything sprouted with such energy and gave such lavish yields that Pero Vaz de Caminha commented in his famous first report on Brazil: "The land is so generous that, if someone wants to take advantage of it, it will produce anything." [2] Regrettably, no one ever wanted to do this, least of all the Portuguese newcomers. The great natural food-producing potential of the land has been badly used or not used at all.

The colonizers discovered early that the soil of the Northeast was marvelously suited to growing sugar cane, and sacrificed all other possibilities of land use to this one crop. But in operating sugar plantations, they almost entirely destroyed the native animal and vegetable life of the region. Food resources were denied and downgraded in the interest of sugar-cane monoculture. This was the result, not so much of an exhaustion of the soil as of a deliberate exploitation of the people.

When they came to Brazil, the Portuguese already knew how to raise sugar cane because the Cape Verdes and the island of Madeira had served as experimental stations. They also knew the ins and outs of the sugar trade, which was then the most promising in the world. They were well aware that profit depended on large-scale production, which required plenty of land, cheap labor and enough capital to ensure a true monopoly. To meet these prerequisites, they brought with them the most abundant supply of capital yet seen in the New World, stepped up the importation of slaves from the coast of West Africa and acquired vast tracts of good land. Once committed to their bold venture, the Portuguese colonizers knew they had to devote themselves body and soul to growing sugar cane or they would fail. Sugar promised immense profits, but it demanded in return nothing less than the enslavement of both men and soil.

It has been said quite rightly that sugar-cane agriculture is self-devouring. The cane eats everything within reach. It pre-empts more and more land, consumes the humus in the soil, annihilates competing crops and meanwhile destroys the very human capital on which it is ultimately based. The history of sugar culture in the Brazilian Northeast, as elsewhere throughout the world, has always been a classic demonstration of the evils of speculative agriculture, an enterprise which may produce initially on a fantastic scale and yield profits beyond the dreams of avarice, but which in the end eats up its own substance. All sugar-growing regions throughout the world have had this self-defeating experience—a phase of rapid growth and transitory splendor is followed by swift and irremediable decay; and the less land available, the quicker the cycle runs its course. The story is identical in the Brazilian Northeast, Cuba, Haiti, Java, Puerto Rico, the Barbados and any other places where sugar has initially been kind.

The small island of Barbados represents a model in which the successive phases of the cycle can be easily seen and analyzed. The Englishman Vincent T. Harlow, whose *History of the Barbados: 1625–1685*[3] is a definitive study of the island's history, points out that at the beginning the colony had a mixed agriculture. The land was divided into small holdings on which cotton, tobacco, citrus fruits, cattle, hogs and other subsistence products were raised. During this early period, 1625–45, living conditions were good, and the English population grew from 1,400 inhabitants in 1628 to 6,000 in 1636 and to 37,000 in 1643. But with the development of sugur cane, introduced around the middle of the seventeenth century by Dutchmen who had fled from the Brazilian Northeast, the original diversification of agriculture was superseded. The small farmsteads were swallowed up by sugar plantations, and food supplies became progressively limited. This led to a mass exodus of white inhabitants. By 1667 there were only 20,000 whites on the island; in 1786 there were 16,000; in 1807 there were 15,500; and today the population is about 15,000. Black slaves replaced white labor. Thus a slaveholding plantation economy developed in Barbados, rose to temporary splendor between 1650 and 1685 and then fell into decline. By this time the island's resources were practically exhausted. The forests, at first so dense that it was hard to find clear space to found a colony,[4] were completely devastated, and the growing of subsistence crops stagnated. Meanwhile, Barbados sugar could no longer be produced cheaply enough to compete in the international market.

That is the history of the sugar cycle in Barbados, as related by Harlow and confirmed in general by other responsible historians. In Jamaica, Trinidad, Cuba and other sugar islands in the West Indies the process was much the same, though the typical cycle was completed more slowly, as may be verified by historical studies of English and Spanish colonization in the Caribbean.[5]

So the Portuguese colonist in Northeast Brazil was not alone in his error. The English in Barbados, the French in Haiti, the Spanish in Cuba made the same mistake of depending on a one-crop sugar economy, and in a way they were even more crushingly dominated by it than the Portuguese. For the Portuguese showed considerable versatility in making the most of what they found and in acclimating new plants and animals. Other colonists were unable to do this as well and failed to take root in the Northeast soil.

The development of a sugar-cane economy, despite the social evils that this plant drew in its wake and despite sugar cane's almost morbid hostility toward other plant species, nevertheless deserves credit for consolidating Portuguese colonization in the tropics. Where other countries had tried to do this sort of thing for a century, their only success had been in establishing simple trading posts on the coasts of Africa, America and the Far East.

As the coastal Northeast was cleared for growing cane almost the entire forest was burnt or cut down. Destruction of the virgin forest was so complete that today, in a region once called the "Northeast forest zone," only scattered remnants of the original woodland remain. By doing away with the tree cover, sugar-cane culture rapidly impoverished the soil. Renewal of the humus formed by the decomposition of vegetable matter was diminished, while erosion was vastly enhanced. In a study of erosion in the Western Hemisphere,[6] Ward Shepard, a former U.S. Department of Agriculture specialist, cites the Northeast of Brazil as one of the areas most seriously afflicted, principally as a result of the immoderate cultivation of sugar cane. Once shorn of its forest mantle, the land fell easy victim to erosion. The many small rivers that cross the Northeast were docile at first and helped the colonist to conquer the land and set up his sugar agronomy. But once the river banks were stripped of trees and the valleys through which the rivers flowed were left naked to the sun, the same waterways became a menace. In flood they tore up the moist soil of the flatlands, dissolved minerals and humus, and washed everything away.

But deforestation did more than impoverish the soil and reduce the agricultural resources. It also all but wiped out the wildlife dependent on the forest.[7] The game which had been abundant during early colonial times practically disappeared. The animals were driven off by burning and clearing and were forced to take refuge in a constantly narrowing habitat. Today few wild creatures are left. The sugar-cane complex devastated regional dietary resources on two fronts: first, it destroyed animals, plants and the soil itself; and second, it militated against the introduction of a subsistence type of agriculture; the planters stubbornly resisted any attempt to use the good land for anything but growing sugar cane.

There can be no doubt that sugar monoculture has been the main factor in debasing the region's dietary standard. Had the Portuguese colonists who settled there been allowed to grow their traditional foods, the situation would have been greatly improved; for the Portuguese diet in the homeland was notable for a relative richness and variety of fruits, vegetables and greens—products of an intensive garden and orchard culture introduced into the Iberian peninsula centuries before by the Arab invaders.

Unfortunately, this Iberian type of balanced diet was unfeasible in one key respect. Its main staple was wheat, and wheat could not be grown in Northeast Brazil. Thus the Portuguese had to fall back on manioc meal, a food containing much less protein, mineral salts and vitamins and greatly inferior to wheat in nutritional value. In an effort to adjust to the exigencies of the new environment, the Portuguese colonizers first sought to encourage the cultivation not only of manioc, but of other native plants grown by the Indians, such as peanuts, pineapples and *aipim*, the sweet cassava. They also tried to introduce plants which they knew from experience elsewhere in the tropics. Thus, to a degree, polyculture was actually attempted, and it should have produced enough food to ensure a healthy diet for the first colonists in the land of Santa Cruz.

But just as in Barbados, these promising beginnings of diversified farming were soon thwarted by the frenzy of sugar-cane monoculture. Manioc plantings were left to the Indians' primitive care as the colonists ceased to be interested in a subsistence use of land.[8] Soon all that was left of fruit culture was the small plantation orchard, where fruit was grown for the exclusive use of the master's family. In effect, the diet of the Brazilian Northeast was deprived very early of what would have been the beneficial influence of the diet of the homeland. It is true that the Indians sought to resist these limitations imposed by the intruders and refused to collaborate in planting cane to make sugar for export. But they were not strong enough to bring about the formation of a new society. All they could do in the face of the pressures of the plantation system was to flee into the forest, vainly attempting to defend their retreat with bow and arrow.

On the other hand, thanks to their native tradition of subsistence farming, the Negro slaves from Africa were more successful in reacting against the monotonous diet imposed by their Portuguese masters. In spite of their brutal uprooting, the Negroes never lost their love of the earth and the instinct to put a plot of land to seed. Disobeying the master's orders, they planted tiny gardens of manioc, sweet potatoes, beans and corn on the sly. This we can verify from the *quilombos*, the fugitive-slave settlements in the backlands. Palmares, the famous "republic" which runaway slaves from the sugar plantations set up under the leadership of Zumbi in the seventeenth century, illustrates very well how completely the Negro adjusted to his new environment. This settlement lasted sixty-seven years, 1630–97, and was broken up only by an expedition from São Paulo, in the cooler and more energetic South of Brazil. At Palmares the Negro took full advantage of his new environment—using the available natural resources and developing whatever new resources he could. One of the principal activities of the Palmares Negroes was subsistence farming, which included such varied crops as corn, sweet potatoes, manioc, bananas and beans.

Regrettably, however, this African agriculture was never stable or broad enough to have a decisive influence on the food economy of the region (as, for example, in Jamaica, where Negroes who revolted against the planters' greed contributed appreciably to the improvment of the islanders' diet). In Brazil the passive resistance of the Indians, the open defiance of the runaway Negro slaves, and the stubborn resistance of the poorer white and mixed-blood colonists were all unable to overcome the oppressive weight of the plantation system. The royal prohibition against growing crops or raising livestock on a subsistence basis[9] was reinforced by the landlords' unlimited authority, thereby guaranteeing the impregnability of slaveholding and patriarchy. The planters were more jealous of their lands than of their women. They thought it would be wasteful to squander their fields by giving them over to crops of Indian or Negro origin, such as manioc, corn, peanuts or beans, rather than the "noble" (and more profitable) cane. Everything bowed to the influence of sugar cane, and the diet of the region became based on manioc meal, which is cheap and easy to grow and makes no great demands on soil, climate or labor.

The sugar plantation, as described earlier, was introduced into Brazil in 1534, along with a land-ownership system based on great feudal grants, or "captaincies," bestowed by King John III of Portugal. Because this archaic system still survives in Brazil, few attempts have ever been made to cope with the nutritional poverty of the Northeast.

Some steps in this direction were taken by the Dutch, whose occupation lasted from 1629 to 1654. The Dutch, and particularly John Maurice of Nassau who arrived in 1637, were struck by the scarcity of food and issued a decree that made it mandatory to plant manioc on all sugar plantations. However, the decree did not have any great economic effect because the Dutch never penetrated into the interior. Other efforts to modify the system of land use in the Northeast have been even more ephemeral. In spite of great technological progress in the sugar industry, which now uses large mills with modern equipment, and in spite of the federal government's efforts to improve the regional economy, the socio-economic framework that ensures nutritional disaster still prevails.

In the *sertão*, the interior scrubland, hunger has a quite different aspect, reflecting a geography and an economy different from that of the Northeast sugarland. Here the main consideration is not chronic hunger conditioned by the habits of daily life; the problem instead is epidemics of starvation that come in the wake of recurrent periods of drought. In normal times in the *sertão* there is relative abundance. But it can deteriorate rapidly into full-scale famine. The prosperous farmer and the common field worker alike often starve to death along with their women and children.

The extensive semiarid zone called the "drought triangle" has a population of roughly 8,000,000 people, who live mainly on corn, which is filled out with other regional products in a highly desirable combination. Aside from painful periods of drought, the people have a balanced diet as well as enough to eat; as a result, a fair percentage have the stamina to survive in times of calamity.

The Northeast back country is exceptional among areas where the diet is based on corn. Similar areas elsewhere in the world are all scenes of hunger and serious nutritional deficiency. This is true, for example, of Central America,[10] which is alarmingly deficient, and of the pellagra regions of Italy and Rumania. Where corn is the staple, misery abounds—with the striking exception of the *sertão* of Northeast Brazil, where other kinds of food compensate for the serious protein and vitamin deficiencies of corn.

Life in the *sertão* is conditioned by the dry, hot climate. Rainfall is scant and irregular. The topography, soil, plants and animals, as well as the whole economic and social life of the region, are all governed by this scarcity of water. Almost everywhere the thin, sandy, stony, semidesert soil is infertile—the product of climatic extremes, of long intervals of unrelieved sunshine interspersed with sudden cloudbursts which break up the sandy rocks and accelerate their disintegration. However, the *sertão* is not entirely covered by decomposed sandstone. In certain places, particularly in hollows and lowlands, there are strips of more fertile clay soils, usually reddish but sometimes even black. These more fertile soils are generally found on alluvial tablelands and in river bottoms,[11] where the composition and the physicochemical qualities are such that the soil retains water and nourishes growing things. But these sections are limited.

The *sertão* may be divided into three more or less distinct kinds of terrain: (1) the *agreste* (Latin *agrestis*, from *ager* field, or scrubland); (2) the *caatinga* (literally "the white forest" in Tupi), dominated by thorny and stunted vegetation and other xerophytic growth; and (3) the high *sertão*, or upland country.

The *agreste* is a transitional strip between the semiarid part of the Northeast where spiny growth abounds and the coastal Northeast of moist and verdant cane fields. There is always some water in this *agreste* subarea. Even in the heat of the summer, rivers there do not dry up entirely; they retain at least a trickle of water or shrink to a series of pools. The vegetation is a scrubby version of the forest found in the humid region.

The *caatinga* is the kingdom of the cactus family and other types of drought-resistant plants. Out of the harsh, dry soil spring the Nery melon cactus (*coroas de frade*) and the Peru cereus (*mandacaru*), bristling with spines. Trees are diminished to the size of bushes, and desert scrub dot the scorched landscape. Here, in the most arid zone of the Northeast, the rivers turn to ribbons of sand in the dry season, their shimmering beds naked to the sun.

In the high *sertão* the climate is not quite so severe. Certain zones have a type of savanna vegetation, and fertile valleys are laced with the rich green of carnauba palms. There are fewer spiny plants, and the droughts are not so pitiless.

The *caatinga*, with the least rainfall of all, is the true heart of the *sertão*. In the *caatinga* only the most rugged kinds of plants survive the periods of extreme dryness. The *agreste* and the high *sertão*, on the other hand, are attenuated forms of the *caatinga*.[12]

Although each of these three subareas is somewhat different geographically and economically, for the purposes of this book they need not be discussed separately. The diet is much the same throughout, and from a nutritional point of view they can be lumped together as the cornstaple area of the Northeastern *sertão*.

As noted, the flora of the whole region is xerophytic, adapted for growth in a hot, dry environment. Trees shrink to mere shrubs for the sake of survival. The fronded cashew of the coast, *Anacardium occidentale,* is replaced on the sandy plateaus of the *caatinga* by the *Anacardium humilis,* or scrub cashew, known locally as the *caju* or *acaju.* To minimize evaporation, the whole mass of the tree, to its very leaves, is stripped to essentials. The trunk is impermeable, and the roots thrust out in all directions to suck up what little moisture is available. It is the same with all plants of the *caatinga;* they survive by limiting their output of energy and storing up water in bulb, root and stem.

Outstanding among these xerophytes are the prickly pear, the Peru cereus, relatives of the old-man or woolly cactus (with the same whitish, hairy appearance) and various torch cactuses, known generically in Brazilian as *facheiro.* Also characteristic of the region are the bromeliads, plants with saber-sharp leaves, such as the cassabanana, the ibiramira bumelia and the *creata,* of which the last has no common English name. All these plants are extremely valuable to both men and animals, since they provide the only source of water during times of severe drought. Recognizing their high water content, the French botanist Saint-Hilaire (1799–1853) called them "vegetable fountains," and another Frenchman, Saint-Pierre (1737–1814), author of *Paul et Virginie,* described them as "springs of the desert."

In areas where the soil is not so thin and dry, there are pod-bearing trees of the acacia family and plants of the bignonia, or trumpet-creeper family. Larger species, such as the Brazilian jujube tree and the hog plum tree, so named because the yellow plumlike fruit is especially liked by pigs, grow in moist depressions and along riverbanks. These trees correspond to the baobabs and acacias of the African bush.[13]

After a rainy period natural pasturelands, thick and continuous in some places, thin and ragged in others, suddenly spring into being. This ephemeral cover (*babugem* in Brazilian) consists of various grasses and other plants. The plants of the *babugem* sprout, flower and seed almost from one day to the next, a kind of "resurrection phenomenon." Within days the whole countryside is transformed from tawny aridity to a bright carpet of flowering green. The *babugem* is analogous to the acheb of the Sahara, which Gauthier has described as follows: "The acheb is not a specific plant, but a collection of plant species with a tactic of their own for resistance to drought. They survive by virtue of the fact that their seeds can withstand desiccation almost indefinitely. When rain comes, the seeds of the acheb respond with amazing energy. In a few days plants sprout, thrust up their stems, brust into flower and throw off seeds. Scattered by the wind, caught in niches in the rocks, these seeds can lie dormant in the sand for ten years, if need be, waiting for the coming of another rain . . ."[14]

In higher places a better soil and somewhat more rain give rise to milder vegetation, of a darker and more succulent green, a water-loving plant cover similar to that of the flood plain.[15] In these upland areas, where altitude reverses the climatic picture, entirely different tree species, many of them bearing edible fruit, are found growing in clumps. Among these are the *mangabeira,* bearing an orange-colored, plumlike fruit usually eaten when overripe. Another is the guava tree, which also bears a plumlike fruit that can be made into a guava paste called *goiabada.* Typical too are shrubs related to the tree myrtles. These islands of verdure are characteristically located on the flanks of the mountains of Araripe, Baturité and Borborema, a region where grapes, peaches, melons and other temperate-zone fruits can be grown.

However, the importance of these small oases of greenery should not be exaggerated. As a whole, the flora of the backlands is less rich than the fruits typical of the forested coastal area. Aside from the hog plum and the souari nut trees, the plants native to the *sertão* usually produce second-rate fruit which is only occasionally eaten in normal times. The fruit of the *ibiramira bumelia*—a small, tough, spiny shrub—and of the jujube, the cactus and the thistle is eaten only under great pressure, during catastrophic droughts when the people in desperation chew the bark from trees and even their hempen sandals. Meanwhile, the palm trees of the high *sertão,* unlike those of the Amazon basin, have little food value. The carnauba, or wax palm, the commonest palm in the region, is very valuable but yields nothing edible—except that in hard times one can eat the roots of the young tree, or *palmito.* It is true, as Euclides da Cunha, author of *Rebellion in the Backlands,* notes, that "in periods of drought a kind of bread is prepared from the shoots of the uricury, or feather palm, after they have been grated and cooked. Unfortunately, this 'bread' is of poor quality, a miserable tortillalike bread or *bró,* which swells and gluts the stomachs of the starving to illusory fullness." [16]

The backlands animals and fish provide little food; the rivers and artificial lakes scattered throughout the region contain far fewer fish than those in the forested areas. Water evaporates at a tremendous rate in this broiling climate, and rains are highly irregular. This occasions wide variations in the salinity of the water, and often makes it unsuitable for aquatic life. Only the year-round rivers like the São Francisco support appreciable numbers of fish. Terrestrial wildlife also contributes very little food, though at least there are no species dangerous to man. Such predators as foxes and hawks, among the latter particularly the caracara, a hawk of vulturelike habit, compete with man for small game and in addition prey on his chickens, goats and sheep.

Birds are abundant, particularly the parrots, most notably the *jandaia,* or yellow-headed parakeet, and a variety of doves. Migratory birds, which pass through the backlands in enormous flocks at certain times of the year, provide the people with a valuable dietary supplement.

Considering the forbidding landscape and limited food supply, we may well wonder what attracted the first pioneers to this region. It was the spirit of adventure, the instinct for liberty described by Capistrano de Abreu, a turn-of-the-century historian and authority on Indian dialects, which led the first Portugese adventurers to penetrate the deep hinterland—that and a greed for gold and precious stones. However, once it became clear that there would be no mines in the Northeast *sertão* and that the land had little agricultural value, the backlands colonists quickly turned their attention to raising cattle. These beasts, brought from Portugal and the Cape Verde Islands, soon made themselves at home in the dry and healthful air and developed very well wherever there was natural pasture.

Domingo do Loreto Coutto, the early-colonial Dominican friar who wrote the famous *Compensations of Brazil and Glories of Pernambuco,* records the way cattle raising developed: "Thirteen kinds of grass serve as pasture for the animals. As a result of this generosity, there are so many cattle and horses in Pernambuco that more than 40,000 are exported each year, despite the vast numbers going to the captaincies. The horses are fast of foot, easy to break in and so strong that, leaving Pernambuco for Minas Gerais with a load of 194 pounds on their backs they will walk some 1300 miles without shoeing and arrive in good condition." The horses and mules of the *sertão* were the only means of transportation through the inhospitable jungle. As for the cattle, entering by way of Pernambuco, they gradually spread through the Northeast backlands and were rafted into the interior along the rivers, particularly the São Francisco, which became the main artery of the hide economy of the Northeast interior.[17]

The big market for cattle that developed early in the coastal and forest region provided an important stimulus for stock raising in the high *sertão.* Demand was great for draft animals to work on the plantations, as well as for meat to feed the growing number of workers on the sugar plantations.

Still another market was created by the rapid growth of mining in the Central states. Down from the North came droves of cattle to feed the people who crowded into the mining areas to the south. In these mining areas there was a shortage of everything and all food had to be brought in from the outside. "With the possible exception of pigs, which live in close relationship with the kitchen, or the collards growing half-wild in the yard, everything needed for the domestic economy is brought in from the outside. The miner's family does not live amid abundance. Exploitive storekeepers charge exorbitant prices, and the mine owner, absorbed in his mining and imagining that there will be plenty of gold to pay for everything, submits to the demands of the dealers." This is from the *As Minas Geraes** of Miran de Barros Latif. Speaking of the same situation another modern authority, Paulo Prado, says: "During the early gold rush period an ox cost as much as 100 *oitavas* [3586 grams, or about 10 ounces] of gold dust, while it could be bought for only an *alqueire* [bushel] of manioc meal. This state of affairs improved only when herds of cattle arrived from Curitiba and stock from the plains of Bahia reached Rio das Velhas." [18]

The food shortage in the mining district, indicated by these exorbitant prices, once again gives evidence of the evil effects of the various forms of economic exploitation successively imposed on the Brazilian people—and all these varying forms reflect a complete indifference to the development of subsistence agriculture. When the California pioneer John Sutter found gold while digging a mill-race, it led to the loss of his ranch, trading post and all his

---

* Here "Minas Geraes" literally means the "general mines" where gold and diamonds were mined. Later "Minas Gerais" was used as the name of the second-most-populous state in Brazil, just south of the Nordeste, where the mines were located.

wealth.[19] The discovery of gold similarly impoverished the Brazilians. People died of starvation beside heaps of gold because farming and stock raising were neglected.

In any case, with two good markets competing for its cattle—the sugar lands of the Northeast and the mining country to the south—the *sertão* prospered. Meanwhile, goat raising was successfully introduced. Goats need less water than cattle and can live on poorer pasture; they can get by on a mountainside or even a rock pile, eating wiry grass or even stems, bark and leaves from shrubs. The Northeast has become the great goat-raising center of the country; the states of Pernambuco and Bahia account for more than 50 per cent of the herd.

Indeed, goats have adjusted so well that they threaten to ruin the land. In a study of deforestation in Ceará, the botanist Loefgren noted that goats run wild in the region: "Goats are another substantial factor in the destruction of the forests, or at any rate a factor making it difficult to preserve the cover of trees and shrubs. Since there are perhaps more goats than cattle on open range in Ceará, it is easy to imagine the damage they cause to the higher vegetation." [20] But though goats may have been hard on the land, at least they have provided meat and milk for the people.

As his herds continued to grow (see the excellent documentation of Fernão Cardim Antonil) the backlands peasant did not succumb, like his fellow Brazilians, to the temptations of monoculture, becoming a rancher to the exclusion of all else. The forested parts of the Northeast, where he sent most of his cattle for sale, offered no regular and adequate food supply in return, and in addition the road was long and difficult. He was led to devote a certain portion of his time to planting subsistence crops. Thus, a healthy form of settlement developed, where the stockman doubled as farmer.

At first the backlands settler, or *sertanejo*, raised crops only for his own use. He was really more gardener than farmer—planting a patch of corn or beans, manioc or sweet potatoes, squash or cucumbers, in the wetter valleys and lowlands or on the flood plains along the river. The plantation owners of the coast, with their far-ranging cane fields, sneered at these "backwoods plots." Nevertheless, this subsistence gardening made a valuable contribution to a better life in the region and provided the backlander with a diversified diet which in normal times was much better than that of the sugar country.

On a basis of cattle raising and subsistence agriculture, plus what he could piece out in game and fish, the backlander adapted his Portuguese cooking methods to the new situation, improvising as he went, and ended up with a regional cuisine. It was a plain but well-balanced diet, a good example of how people can make even a poor environment yield the basic necessities.

The *sertanejo* made corn his staple, the main calorie base and supplier of energy. But to escape the typical inadequacies of a corn diet, he combined this staple with other foods. In the backlands corn is almost always eaten in combination with milk, which supplements its low protein content. Two typical dishes are *angu*—a thick porridge of corn flour with milk and salt, though sometimes manioc or rice flour is substituted, and at times water for milk—and *canjica*, a combination of hominy grits and milk.

At the Institute of Nutrition at the University of Brazil,

experiments to determine the nutritive value of this combination of corn and milk showed that rats developed better
when fed with this mixture than when proteins were provided solely by corn.[21] However, it is not only with corn that
milk is consumed in large quantities in the backlands. Milk
is drunk with morning coffee and eaten in the form of fresh
or cured clabber as well as butter or cheese. Most frequently it is eaten as *requiejão*, a kind of curd cheese that
can be taken raw or roasted. Even in South and West Central Brazil, where cattle abound, milk is not used either
alone or in combination as much as in the Northeast backlands. Though more milk is produced in the South, it is
largely sold in the cities, which are linked to the grazing
lands by easy means of transportation.

But in the Northeast the *sertanejo* is still pretty much
cut off from the urban markets, and to this day most milk,
butter and cheese are consumed locally. Milk is part of the
two morning meals, which might be, for example, *angu* or
couscous (a stiff pudding) with milk. It is also used in more
pretentious dishes like meat and squash and in such des-
serts as the celebrated *umbuzada,* made of hog plum and
particularly rich in proteins and vitamins. *Umbuzada*
brings to mind the milk-and-date combinations eaten by the
nomads of the Sahara, who appear to thrive.[22]

Besides milk the *sertanejo* has a liberal source of proteins in beef, mutton and kid meat, butchering stock for his
private use. Beans, manioc meal, sweet potatoes, yams, a
crude brown sugar called *rapadura* and coffee are other
foods which he eats regularly. He likes many kinds of
beans, though in smaller quantities than corn, and this further increases his total protein consumption—which still is

not fully adequate.[23] Very little bread is eaten, and carbo-
hydrates are supplied primarily by corn and sweet potatoes.[24]

The paucity of fruit is an obvious defect in the backlands diet. As remarked earlier, nature offers little in the
way of fruit, and the farmer, who is always threatened by
periodic drought, has never been inclined to plant or-
chards. The soil and climate are not entirely unamenable to
this kind of agriculture, but the risk is heightened by the
fact that fruits require a longer growing period than crops
such as corn, manioc and beans, which mature quickly.

Since he grows no fruit of his own, the *sertanejo* must
turn to the limited varieties he can find in the wild—the hog
plum, the ambarella or Otaheite apple and the fruit of the
ibiramira bumelia. Because some wild fruits are poisonous, they are all approached cautiously. There is a supersti-
tion, for example, that fruit should be eaten only in the
morning; in the afternoon it may give you fever, and if
eaten at night, may be fatal. Meanwhile, the consumption of
vegetables is limited to squash, gherkins and onions, with
coriander as a popular seasoning.

In sum, generally the *sertanejo* has enough to eat, if
nothing to spare. But when drought comes, hunger stalks
the *sertão* and all forms of life in the *caatinga* wither away.
People and animals, domestic and wild, migrate or die.
Drought in the *sertão* is a familiar subject in Brazilian literature and has impressed foreigners as well. The Germans
J.B. von Spix and C.F.P. von Martius, who explored Brazil,
1817–20, and crossed the Bahia *sertão* during a dry spell,
wrote in their *Travels in Brazil:* "This scorching desert
seems to be bereft of all green things. The only life or

movement that we saw was in the termite nests, which rise in cones as much as five feet high. Birds and mammals seemed to have migrated to better-watered regions." [25]

Crops vanish from the fields; the seeds are left buried in parched dust and the tender young plants turn black and dessicated. The dry pasture becomes dust and is carried away by hot winds, leaving the cattle without food or water. To save as much of the herd as they can, the cowhands feed the cattle cactus, burning off the spines and hacking up the trunks into manageable segments. Where the starved cattle run free on the open range, they try unaided to get at the pulpy cactus, tearing their mouths and hoofs in the process.[26] It is in vain. In the end they die. The farmyards, fields and gray wastes of *caatinga* become boneyards littered with bleaching carcasses.

The backlander seldom has any reserves to fall back on. First, he limits his consumption of food to beans, a little corn and manioc meal. Next, he turns to roots, seeds and the fruit of whatever wild plants survive. This forced diet includes many substances unthinkable for human consumption elsewhere and largely indigestible. Some have a strange taste, some are irritants. Few have any nutritive value. They serve only to ease the pangs of hunger for an hour or two by filling the stomach with cellulose.

By the time the backlander begins eating these unpalatable substances, he has reached the end of his tether. The next move is to flee the *sertão*, become a refugee, a Brazilian *retirante*. Then, interminable files of drought victims wind along the dusty roads like a human centipede. Men, women and children straggle on, "deformed by nutritional disturbances, blackened skin glued to their long skeletons, fleshless and stinking from the body's consumption of its own tissue." [27]

The drought victim sometimes walks hundreds of miles in search of relief. With a few handfuls of meal and a chunk of coarse brown sugar, carrying on his back the smaller children and a hammock to sleep in, the *sertanejo* wanders across endless miles of semidesert tableland, resigned to whatever may come. Without resources, passing through an absolutely impoverished countryside, using his last energies on the march, the refugee only adds to his misfortunes by flight. In eyewitness accounts of unusually severe droughts, such as those in 1744, 1790, 1846, 1877, 1932 and 1958, we find the *retirante* in all stages of physical exhaustion, starving to death by the roadside.

Only in recent years, with the growth of airline traffic over the Brazilian interior and the resulting hourly checks on air-mass movements, have the dynamics of the Brazilian climate become at least broadly understood. This new scientific knowledge throws some light on the droughts.

First, during the Brazilian winter (the American summer), the Northeast is dominated by stable air masses which originate over the South Atlantic and flow northward over the Central Highland. These air masses lose their moisture before arriving over the Northeast.

However, in the Brazilian summer (the American winter), moist, violently unstable air masses from the Caribbean and other low latitudes of the North Atlantic push down toward Brazil. The coastal strip gets most of their moisture. But now and then the warm front moves deeper inland in a great bow, sometimes getting as far in as Ceará. When this happens there are sudden cloudbursts. But the warm front quickly disintegrates and may not return for months, or years, at least not in any force. Then there is searing drought as the sun shines on, week after week, month after month.

Some parts of the backlands, get an annual average of twenty to twenty-five inches of rain, others only ten. But it must be borne in mind that much of this rain is most likely concentrated in a few days, sometimes in a single day. Such a downpour gullies the slopes, washes away the topsoil and damages the riverbanks.

Drought is by no means the Northeast's only defect, though the pressure it exerts on the people is tremendous. It is a specter that lurks forever. Today about 4,000,000 Northeasterners have neither land nor work: they make up a migrant labor force constantly in search of employment. It is not unusual for 200,000 of them to move South in a single year. When drought strikes, panic accelerates the outward trek. It is hard enough to endure life in the Northeast in good years—when the farm laborer earns an annual wage of thirty dollars. When drought is added to chronic deprivation, the resulting agony can scarcely be imagined.

Hunger victims become shockingly thin. The face gets dry, withered and sucked in, the eyes stare out of deep sockets, the flesh of the cheeks disappears, the bony framework protrudes under the thin, blackened skin. Even people who are normally lean lose as much as half their weight.

But this is not all. Victims of chronic nutritional deficiencies are common too in grotesque variations. It is the children who are the most spectacularly affected by deficiency diseases; they stop growing and even regress. Felipe Guerra reports that in the great drought of 1773 "children who were already walking returned to the creeping stage." [28] Many are marked for life if they survive the drought and the famine that follows it. They remain dwarfish, their bones and flesh deformed by hunger and glandular disturbances—an ugly and pitiful contrast to the generally stalwart backlanders' physique.

In addition to the stunting effect, protein deficiencies cause swollen bellies. Edematous conditions, both mild and dropsical, are one of the commonest sights during a drought in the Northeast. Among the refugees there are always hideous figures on toothpick legs with huge bellies swollen by dropsy—the dropsical gut gives a nightmare impression of having eaten to satiety.

Reduced to this parlous state, drought victims lose the capacity to resist disease. Their aimless flight, during which they lack the least rudiments of hygiene, becomes a veritable death march. They eat polluted food and pollute everything around them with their excreta. They have no water to wash, and their crowding together increases the chances of contracting a contagious disease. A popular poet described the *retirada* in this fashion:

Let us march on and face
Thirty thousand epidemics,
Cold, dropsy,
Which no one can escape.
Those who go to the lowlands
Die of the epidemic,

Those who stay in the *sertão*
Go hungry every day.*

Those who survive the march and reach country where
there is water are in most cases attacked by serious infectious diseases and die by the thousands. In the historic
droughts of Northeast Brazil starvation is always followed
by epidemics. In the drought of 1877 the refugees from the
backlands of Ceará who piled up in the provincial capital
of Fortaleza were all but exterminated by smallpox, yellow
fever and dysentery. Of a total Fortaleza population of
124,000, there were 80,000 cases of smallpox. "Yellow
fever, beriberi, dropsy, dysentery and smallpox filled the
cemeteries to overflowing in that terrible year of 1878,"
says Rodolfo Teófilo. "In the city of Fortaleza, during a
period of 12 months, 56,791 people were buried in the
cemeteries of São João Batista and Lagea Funda, an appalling mortality for a population of 124,000." Thus epidemics all but depopulated the city, and drought extended its
malign effects as far as the coast.

Another report on losses suffered during the same 1877
drought, transcribed by Edmar Morel in his interesting
documentary on Padre Cícero of Joazeiro, reveals the following figures: "The 19th century saw ten great winters and
seven great droughts. Of these the one in 1845 was ex-

* Marchemos a encarar
Trinta mil epidemias
Frialdade, hidropisia
Que ninguém pode escapar
Os que para o brejo vão
Morrem de epidemia
Sofrem fome todo dia
Os que ficam no sertão.[29]

tremely hard on the cattle, and the one in 1877–79 has become famous. The latter resulted in the death of 500,000 inhabitants of Ceará and neighboring areas, or about 50 per cent of the population. In most great droughts, however, the loss of life is usually no more than 33 per cent. Of the dead in 1877–1879, it has been calculated that 150,000 died of outright starvation, 100,000 from fever and other diseases, 80,000 from smallpox and 180,000 from poisonous or otherwise harmful food, from starvation or from thirst alone." [30]

Of the refugees who fled from the drought-stricken backlands to the Amazon region, attracted by the mirage of making fortunes in rubber collecting and planting, it has been estimated that 500,000[31] died from epidemics, malaria, worm infestations and beriberi. This flight from Ceará occurred during the 1870's and 1880's. At its height people from Ceará poured into the Amazon region at the rate of 20,000 a year. A few returned, but most perished. They arrived in the green hell of the rain forest without any reserves of vitamins. At home in the Northeast they had not succumbed to beriberi for the good reason that there they had not eaten much of anything, but their diet in the Amazon, based on canned foods and manioc meal, was much more abundant and at the same time grossly out of balance. Their bodies could not stand up under this assault, and the result was beriberi and multiple neuritis, which accompanies it. The Amazon region, and the Acre territory in particular, became a great sinkhole of suffering and death. "Acre is like another world; it may be fine, but nobody who goes there ever comes back," sadly observes a character in *A Bagaceira* (*The Bagasse Shed*), the backlands novel by

José Américo de Almeida.[32] And then, in the end, the same character himself sets off, fatefully compelled, for the green hell.

Thus the *retirantes* are decimated by their peregrinations. Survivors drift to the coastal cities. Some keep an ear cocked for word of the first rains, then return to their native soil and the eternal cycle of drought and reprieve. Others stay on and become marginal populations in the capitals of the Northeast. In Recife, for example, amid the mangrove swamps of the Capiberibe River, a slum city has grown up, to which each new drought adds a new settlement of refugee shacks raised on stilts above the swamps. Here the migrant backlander lives in maladjustment and defeat, beset by chronic dietary deficiencies.

Around Fortaleza there are people who are if anything more miserable, some of whom barely survive by eating wild greens, such as the common purslane and the panicled flameflower, these cooked with salt and eaten with the amphibious flask snail, the *arua*. Meanwhile, hunger undermines the *sertanejo*'s spirit as well as his body. Under pressure from the necessity to eat, primal instincts come to the fore. A famished man, like any other hungry animal, ceases to behave and think in his normal fashion.[33]

As for the wildlife of the *sertão*, drought throws it completely out of joint. In the memoirs of Father Joaquim José Pereira,[34] an eighteenth-century vicar in Rio Grande do Norte, we read that in the drought of 1792 a large number of bats appeared and attacked people and animals even in the daytime. This fact is confirmed by Rodolfo Teófilo, who writes that "a plague of bats, known in all the droughts, but especially in the drought of 1792, began to appear, causing damage in certain parts of the province." Thus we see how hunger drove a normally nocturnal animal to such a pitch that it began to move about in daylight and even dared to attack man. Infestations of rattlesnakes are also common after severe droughts. Normally these snakes, typically the *jararacucu*, a pit viper like the American fer-de-lance, keep very much to themselves.

"After the great drought of 1877 a terrible evil developed throughout the province. 'Rattlesnakes' devastated the *sertões* in the most fearful way. These terrible reptiles appeared in such abundance that sometimes 500 of them were killed at a time. Men and cattle surviving the drought ran the risk of losing their lives through poisonous bites." So writes Virgilio Brigido in the preface to *A Fome (Hunger)* by Rodolfo Teófilo. Although Roquette Pinto thinks the cause of rattlesnake scourge was that due to the great heat, more eggs were hatched, it is my impression that the infestation resulted simply from hunger, which drove the snakes from their dens and sent them, mad for food, along the roads and into corrals, yards and even farmhouses.

In other famines responsible observers have noted strange aberrations in the behavior of starving animals, wild and domestic. Pedro y Pons reports that in the famine in Barcelona during the Spanish Civil War, 1936–39, stray dogs multiplied and became a menace in the streets. In his *Enfermidades por Insuficiência Alimentícia (Diseases from Lack of Food)* he writes: "Any reasonably observant person could not fail to see the dogs in the streets anxiously searching for food. Some were dried up, with their ribs sticking out, others were puffed and bloated, with a tired gait and mangy coat, and frequently with paralysis of one back foot."

A report to the Smithsonian Institution in Washington on the 1913 drought in the Waterberg region of the African Transvaal noted striking changes in wild-animal behavior: "Many nocturnal carnivores now hunt by day, and the leopards, contrary to habit, attack camps in the afternoon. The baboons, which formerly never moved about in the dark, now seem not to sleep any more at all, but forage for food night and day. Wild dogs have become extremely aggressive . . ."

And under the threat of starvation, man too is capable of drastic changes in behavior. "When a calamity descends upon us, our sensations and perceptions, our sense organs, tend to become extremely sensitive to all the phenomena of the calamity and to all objects and facts related to it," writes the Harvard sociologist Pitirim A. Sorokin.[35] The nervous irritability may reach the stage of madness. Navigators of the sixteenth and seventeenth centuries were quite familiar with this sort of thing, and called it "hunger hydrophobia." There is a curious report on these nervous states in the *Histoire d'un voyage fait en la terre du Brésil* (*History of a Voyage Made to the Land of Brazil*) of Jean de Lery, a French Huguenot shoemaker who went to Brazil in the late 1540–50's. Telling about his trip home to Europe in 1558, he says: "The food ran out completely at the beginning of May, and two sailors died of hunger hydrophobia. They were buried at sea according to custom." And then he goes on to say: "During such outright starvation the body becomes exhausted, nature swoons, the senses are alienated, the spirit fades away and this not only makes people ferocious but provokes a kind of madness, thus justifying the popular saying that someone is 'going mad from hunger,' meaning that someone is suffering from lack of food."

The sensations which arise from hunger are intermittent, and there are periodic exacerbations and remissions. At first hunger produces an abnormal nervous excitement and extreme irritability. The sense perceptions become unusually sharp and fasten on any possiblity of getting food to appease the relentless hunger. The visual sense achieves an incredible level of acuity, even while the famished organism is failing.

Note this description of drought victims by a writer from the Northeast: "More dead than alive. Only the eyes alive, piercingly alive. Pupils reflecting the sun of the droughts. Eyes reveal spasms of panic, as though terrified of themselves. Agonized concentrations of flashing vitality." [36] In effect, man reverts to the predatory, and his hunger-sharpened eyes pierce distances in search of a victim. "The predatory animal," Spengler writes, "is the supreme form of mobile life; it represents the maximum of liberty, with respect both to others and to itself, the maximum of responsibility and solitude, the extreme necessity of asserting itself by fighting, conquering and annihilating." [37] And it is when he is starving that the backlander becomes an insuperable hunter, sensing in the slightest movement of a leaf or the almost imperceptible sound the frightened tinamou, or Brazilian "partridge," hidden in the bumelia thicket, or the famished cavy crouched among the rocks. He also turns to banditry.

In a penetrating essay on the art of hunting, which

serves as a preface to the Conde de Yebes' *Veinte Años de Caça Mayor* (*Twenty Years of Big Game Hunting*), Ortega y Gasset points out that one of the basic conditions of hunting is the scarcity of game. "The fact that hunting is universal," says Ortega, "presupposes that little game exists now or has ever existed. If game were abundant, there would be no reason for the peculiar behavior among animals, including man, that we call the art of hunting." [38] He then goes on to show that the hunter depends mostly on his visual sense.

Explorers and pioneers who have experienced starvation have left a richly detailed documentation of the obsessions of the hungry man who is bent on getting something to eat.[39] After this phase of exaltation comes one of apathy, depression, nausea and difficulty in concentrating. Knut Hamsun describes these cyclical emotional crises in his autobiographical novel, *Hunger*. His hero passes from extreme irritability to morbid quiescence. He is, in one mood after the other, irascible, gentle, perverse, magnanimous— all without apparent reason. This psychic rhythm, which is so common during periods of famine in the backlands, must be what certain authors had in mind when they described the *sertanejo* as "cyclothymic," or manic-depressive; [40] that is, someone keyed to the extreme demands of his environment.

Yet in many other respects he is schizoid. His tendency toward isolation and his exaggerated feeling for liberty suggest the schizothyme rather than the cyclothyme. Carried to pathological extremes, these schizothymic temperaments (the opposite of cyclothymic in Ernst Kretschmer's typology), become on the one hand the bloodthirsty *cangaceiro*, or backlands bandit, and on the other hand the fanatic visionary. It is my impression that the schizothymic type, the introvert, dominates in the *sertão*. And his extreme forms of behavior, in final analysis, are an exteriorization or projection of a tremendous inner conflict between the feral impulses and instincts of hunger and his normally civilized desires and aspirations—a struggle between the human and the predatory, the angel and the demon, which is rooted in the inherent ambivalence of the human being. Even under the best conditions the *sertanejo* lives under pressure. It is not strange that when he is starving, his personality should break down and run wild.

This complete transformation is easily observed among the *vaqueiros,* or cowboys, who are typical inhabitants of the region. The *vaqueiro* of the Northeast is generally a serious and scrupulously honest man. He is capable of taking care of a lost animal for years while waiting for its legitimate owner to show up and claim it. *Rebellion in the Backlands* examines this type of personality: "Should a strange animal with a brand he knows show up in his corral, he will promptly return it to its owner. Otherwise he will keep the intruder and care for it as he does for the others, but he will not take it to the annual fair, nor will he use it for any kind of labor, for it does not belong to him. Indeed, he would rather let it die of old age. If a cow gives birth to a calf, he brands the calf with the same unknown brand, displaying a perfection of artistry in doing so; and he will repeat the process with all its descendants . . . he adheres strictly to his strange contract, which no one has written or even suggested."

All this flows from the cowman's iron honesty. Also, so Xavier de Oliveira tells us, when an animal with an unknown brand becomes unmanageable and starts breaking down fences and destroying crops, the farmers of the neighborhood first determine its value, then butcher it and divide it up according to the share figured for each. When the owner appears, he is given the exact amount at which the beast was assessed. This honorable way of dealing is typical of the ancient moral code of the backlands.[41] Yet these same people resort to stealing cattle or goats when the drought strikes. In a delirium of hunger Chico Bento, a character in *O Quinze* (*The Drought in the Year 1915*), lost all his moral scruples, and "with trembling hands, his throat dry and his eyes bloodshot," clubbed down whatever stray animal crossed his path as he fled the land. Similar lapses from the moral norm often mark the beginning of a life of banditry; in a land of such rigid principles there is no return from the path of error, and transgression is never forgotten.

When starvation has drugged the conscience, conflict rages and true situational psychoses may develop, in accord with what Sorokin has described as "the diversification and polarization of affects." Activated by drought and famine, both saints and bandits arise, and both types can be merged in the same personality. Such a phenomenon was the celebrated fratricide Bento da Cruz de Joazeiro, who, "with a cross in one hand and a dagger in the other," meted out justice in his village. Similarly, in the famous 1897 peasant rebellion in Canudos, truculent Batistas served as aides-de-camp to the fanatically religious Antonio Conselheiro. The Batistas, Euclides da Cunha tells us, were "capable of loading their death-dealing blunderbusses with rosary beads."

We may think of the *cangaceiro*, or bandit, as a personality in which the baser impulses released by hunger have
won the upper hand over normal restraints. The religious
fanatic, on the other hand, represents a victory of the abnormal exaltations of hunger. He is a man who has beat a
retreat into the metaphysical. But both forms of escape—
toward brute force or the metaphysical illusion—are distortions from which no good comes.

In analyzing the factors that helped determine the character of bandit fanatic Antonio Conselheiro, Euclides da
Cunha, in *Rebellion in the Backlands*, places major emphasis on the lack of food. Hunger had made an ascetic of da
Cunha, in *Rebellion in the Backlands*, places major empha-
hunger, thirst, bodily weariness, repressed anguish and
deep-seated misery . . . Many times he came near death
in his prolonged fastings, with a refinement of asceticism
which would have astonished a Tertullian, that somber pro-
pagandist of the doctrine of the gradual elimination of the
physical." Gustavo Barroso, whose *Terra de Sol* (*Land of
the Sun*) is a study of the life and personality of the backlander, also notes how periodic hunger helps fashion the
cangaceiro personality. "The backlands," Barroso writes,
"were watered for many years in succession by fruitful
winters and supplied by abundant harvests. During this period of plenty not a single bandit appeared. The ones
driven from the neighborhoods were hunted out of sight.
But then came the droughts. The farmers fled to the towns,
migrated to the Amazon or became miserable goatherds.
The land lay waste and abandoned. The *cangaceiro* came in
from the outside and settled down, or was recruited from
the ruined people themselves." [42] Afonso Arinos, who is re-

membered for his posthumous *Lendas e Tradições Brasileiras* (*Brazilian Legends and Traditions*), had the same thing in mind near the beginning of this century, when he wrote: "In periods of social instability, provoked by causes of an economic nature . . . the human type known in the Northeast as the *cangaceiro*, or bandit, comes to the fore, and begins to dominate the imagination and, to considerable degree, the popular life of the region." [43]

This is not meant to imply that famine alone creates asocial types. Actually, many other factors have a hand in molding such natures. Nevertheless, there can be no doubt that bandits flourish in times of cataclysm.

In two recent studies,[44] the French sociologist Roger Bastide,* who lived in Brazil for many years, has sought to analyze the bandit-zealot complex of the Northeast. He says that the bandit and the religious fanatic are unquestionably related to the periodic droughts and famines of the Nordeste. He believes also that in the case of religious fanaticism the causal relationship is clearer.

In any case, it is obvious that famine is bound to be connected with a general breakdown of the regional economy, a fear-ridden and despairing environment inviting the rise of the bandit-zealot type of popular leader, who offers either panaceas or revenge against the delinquent establishment. In such troubled times there is a natural predisposition to accept and adore this peculiar type (e.g., Antonio

* Bastide is remembered for his curious paper, *Psicologia do Cafuné* (*Psychology of the Cafuné*), in which *cafuné* means the custom among *sertanejos* of softly snapping one's fingernails on someone's head to express affection, or patting a person's head to soothe him, or abstractedly scratching a dog behind the ears to please him and at the same time soothe and please oneself.

Conselheiro of the Canudos rebellion)—people who symbolize the common urge to escape from misery by force of arms or by magic. Because of this "messianic" connection, the backlanders seldom view the bandit as a vicious criminal; he is more likely thought of as a Robin Hood, celebrated in song as a brave man who lays down his life in knightly fashion to defend the oppressed and feed the hungry, who steals from the rich to give to the poor.

The connection between hunger and mysticism is so well known that it merits only passing comment. Everyone knows that the great religious leaders—Moses, Jesus, Mahomet—preached the virtues of fasting, both to heighten the mystic sensibilities and to develop in their followers a greater propensity for mystic adoration. It is no coincidence that the famine-ridden Middle Ages was a period of mysticism, a time when the masses were alternately seized by a "stupid and hopeless apathy" [45] and by intense mystic fervor that moved them to throw themselves without second thought into deadly religious wars.

And one must remember that until very recently the spirit of the Middle Ages persisted in the backlands in a quite literal sense. The first Portuguese settlers, who came there in the sixteenth century, lived in an atmosphere saturated in medievalism (see Sánchez Albornoz's study of Iberian colonization in South America[46]). The whole way of life of these people was characteristically medieval, at once religious and warlike, mystical yet shamelessly greedy, in striking contrast to the relatively moderate, bourgeois spirit of English colonization in North America. If, as Albornoz claims, the struggle against Islam retarded Spain's and Portugal's emergence from medievalism for centuries, Portugal—immured in "geographic exile, separated from the larger world by the thick wall of the hard and arid Castilian tableland" [47]—was by far the more laggard.

The above exposition of the sufferings of the backlands peasant may clarify to some degree the present political turmoil and explosive tensions of the Northeast. But one should never make the mistake of imagining that climate and geography alone can explain the current situation. The periodic recurrence of drought merely precipitates disaster that was inherent in a highly defective social and economic structure. As we shall see.

chapter 3

THE
FIRST
DISCOVERY

THE first discovery of Brazil, in 1500, passed almost unnoticed, overshadowed by more illustrious exploits of Portuguese navigation. The discovery of Brazil was incidental to the more immediate objectives of Portuguese exploration, since their obsessive dream at that time was to find a sea route to the Orient. Products of the Far East, imported through Arab merchants, had enriched other European countries, and Portugal wanted to share in the wealth. Forced off course by ocean currents and contrary winds, Pedro Alvares Cabral came upon the terra incognita of Brazil, but he limited this stopover to "refreshing" his ships before continuing his voyage in search of the East

Indies. Nevertheless, he sent a report to the king of Portugal, the celebrated letter of Preo Vaz de Caminha and first document of Brazilian history. But the letter made no great impression, and except for a few royal concessionaires who came across the Atlantic on occasion to cut brazilwood for use in the dying trade (brazilwood then being the only visible form of wealth in the new country), Brazil was practically ignored for another thirty years. Before Cabral's discovery, Brazilian life was one of "peace and tranquillity"; at least, so we are told by an early chronicler, the Huguenot Jean de Lery, one of the first to record native life in Brazil before the arrival in full force of conquerors from across the sea.

Land was held in common, and there was no private property. The Indians owned houses and fine lands "in quantities far beyond their needs," Lery tells us. "As regards division of the land, each family head chooses a few acres wherever he wishes and plants his crops; and as for matters of inheritance and boundary quarrels, such problems are left to the misers and lawsuit-mongers of Europe." [1]

The crews of Cabral's fleet, when they had dropped anchor some fifty years before, must have come to similar conclusions about the tranquillity and peacefulness of the natives: "They came all stalwart up to the boat, and Nicolau Coelho made a sign to them to put down their bows, and they put them down," reports Pero Vaz de Caminha in his letter to King Dom Manuel.

After initial contact had been made, very little time was required to lay the basis for a mutual understanding and to engage in barter. "For rattles or other trinkets they [Cabral's people] had with them, they got red parrots, very large and beautiful, and two small green ones, and hoods of green feathers and a kind of cloth woven of many-colored feathers, sufficiently handsome." Also by barter the white men got everything they needed to "refresh" their ships. "They carried as much of this wood as they could with a very good will, and brought it to the boats, and they moved about more gently and surely among us than we did among them."

For many years afterward this method of "redeeming" the wealth of the land (as trading by barter was called) and of enlisting the help of native labor was completely effective. This was the way the ship *Bretoa* was loaded with cargo eleven years after Brazil was discovered, and the same procedure must have been followed by earlier ships, though we have few written details. The Portuguese and French, who worked up and down the coast from Cabo Frio to Cabo São Roque during this early period, devastated the forests to get the logs of brazilwood (from Portuguese *brasa*, glowing coals) for which the country was named; and in dealing with the natives, removing their wood, they needed methods no more persuasive than the offer to exchange a few handfuls of trinkets.

Some well-known historians have described the Indians of early colonial times as hostile and unapproachable. But the success of the first bartering operations would seem to indicate just the opposite.

According to what has come down to us, the Indians had already passed beyond the upper stage of savagery and arrived at the lower stage of barbarism, in Lewis Morgan's terminology. They knew how to make pots and weave nets;

and when they were not on the move, they practiced a rudimentary agriculture based on manioc and corn, from which they obtained a number of foods, particularly manioc meal, a food requiring a relatively complicated preparation. Their cannibalism, of which the conquistadors made so much, seems to have been on the decline. For most part it was restricted to mere ritual, and in some areas prisoners were apparently spared.

It is difficult to determine the development and extent of slaveholding practices among the Indians during these early years. But we do know that tales of Indian slaveholding were exaggerated to make slavery appear to be an Indian tradition and not the white man's invention. Similarly, stories of cannibalism were exaggerated in order to excuse the conquistadors' capture and enslavement of Indians as an act of retribution.

A clarification of this controversial subject, which is not as obscure as may first appear, is very important, I feel, for an understanding of the historical genesis of the Brazilian colonial character.

Is it possible that before the white man's arrival the Brazilian Indians had advanced on their own initiative from the practice of eating their prisoners to enslaving them? It does not seem very likely. A more likely hypothesis is that slavery was introduced after the first contact between white man and Indian, before or after Cabral, but that it had not developed to any great extent, since Indian life had not reached a stage where slavery was worthwhile.

There are stories, of Padre Nóbrega among others, about Indians selling fellow Indians to the Portuguese in Pôrto Seguro; and there are reports of cases in which the natives, under the pressure of hunger or natural calamity, voluntarily sold themselves into slavery. But these seem to refer to occasional and scattered events; and significantly, these incidents came late in the story, at a time when "civilization" had already penetrated some native communities. Also of later origin are tales of Indian war parties for the purpose of taking prisoners and selling them as slaves to the colonists.

Undoubtedly, slavery arises in human history along with civilization, after a society has become sedentary and begun to use prisoners of war for forced labor. But it is doubtful that this can have happened in Brazilian prehistory, before the Indians had attained a fully settled way of life and learned how to domesticate animals and use metals.

It should also be noted that the Portuguese took great care to keep the Indians ignorant of many civilized customs and techniques. For example, in the hinterland, some distance from the coast, they forbade white settlers to smelt metals because they feared the natives might learn the process and put it to dangerous use, making arms and tools of their own.

The relatively short duration of direct barter in trading with the Indians is another argument against an indigenous system of slavery. If Cabral's fleet had found ample supplies of human merchandise—for slaves were a staple commodity among the overseas traders—the early chronicles would have made greater mention of the fact when they referred to trade relations. Had numbers of slaves been readily available, as in West Africa, it would have encouraged an expansion of trade and the continuation of peaceful relations between the Portuguese and the aborigines. But actually, as the chronicles emphasize, the wars which the whites waged against the Indians in order to enslave them coincided with a decline in trade. Why would the colonists have needed to mount bloody slave raids if they could simply have bartered cheap trinkets and bits of bright cloth for already enslaved prisoners of war? The scale and ferocity of these raids demonstrate that reserves of enslaved Indians were scarce or nonexistent among the tribes—getting Indian slaves was impossible except by violence.

As long as the bulk of trade was in forest products, the main concern of the Portuguese was to keep peace with the natives. The captains of Cabral's fleet conferred and decided that "they should not take anyone here by force, or create any scandal, but should do everything to tame and pacify them [the Indians]." It was a counsel of prudence. The captains of other ships landing in Brazil, including the *Bretoa*, must have acted pretty much the same way. At this time it was the mother country's policy to make the Indians the principal source of labor in obtaining raw materials. Trinkets, playing cards and knickknacks would pay them for cutting and preparing the brazilwood, transporting it aboard ship and supplying everything else necessary to the convoys. During the early period of Portuguese occupation Indian labor was also used on the croplands around the "factories."

Thus the conquistadors respected, at least to some degree, the communal-property system that was characteristic of Brazilian prehistory. This relationship with the Indians apparently lasted until 1532, when the institution of great royal land grants, or captaincies, was introduced. From then on, the enslavement of the Indians, previously only occasionally and clandestinely pursued, became commonplace and spread to all regions. Eventually slaves became one of the most profitable commodities, whether for sale or for use on one's own plantation. It is ironic to note in retrospect that Frei Vicente do Salvador (historian of the late sixteenth and early seventeenth century, born in Bahia in 1564), recounted that when the Indian slaving raids were started many of the colonists were not convinced that this was the most efficient way of procuring a labor supply. "Wars," objectors said, "would drive the Indians away," far from the coast. They believed it would be better to "bring them in by peaceful means and by the persuasion of halfbreeds, who knew the language and would use their blood relatives to bring them in more easily than by force of arms."

Throughout the time of the land grants, which witnessed a transition from peaceful to violent dealings with the Indians, trade languished. The skill and cunning of the coastal merchants and the traders trained in the Indies to deal with aborigines was not sufficient to maintain a peaceful coexistence; the Indians and the Portuguese became mutually inimical.

Furthermore, new motivations came into play. With the advent of the captaincy system of colonization it was no longer simply a question of bartering raw materials from the natives and shipping them to the European market, but of clearing and working the land itself. Into this endeavor the most enterprising members of the Portuguese nobility now threw themselves. Conquest was succeeded by serious efforts at colonization. To accomplish their mission of put-

ting the land to work, the colonizers undertook to impose
their will upon the native population, expropriate the Indians' land and goods, force Portuguese ideas down their
throats and in general transform them into docile agents.
The development of the conquered territory into a true colony required new legal institutions and new forms of land
ownership which could flourish only when primitive institutions had been eliminated.

The hunt for Indian slaves did not at first lead to a complete rupture between the natives and the conquistadors.
This was to come later, irremediably, with the large-scale
seizure of Indian lands. It is a commonplace to find in "his-
tories of the various captaincies examples of European and
native populations living together on excellent terms,"
Paulo Merea notes.[2] He explains, however, that this state of
affairs did not result from the "natural way of being" so
much as from the fact that at this point the Portuguese were
still to some degree pursuing peaceful means of co-
operation with the Indians.

A logical reconstruction of this initial period of Brazilian history shows that the duality of method in dealing
with the natives—now by force, now by peaceful means, a
duality which was to continue for a long time—almost certainly reflected a conflict of interest and outlook among
castes and factions in the homeland, a conflict which divided and undermined all sixteenth-century Portugal.

At the time when Brazil was discovered, the agrarian-
minded Portuguese monarchy,[3] whose mentality had been
retarded for centuries by the interminable struggle against
Islam, was still living in the Middle Ages. This fact is fully
documented by such reliable historians as Claudio Sánchez

Albornoz,[4] in his study of Iberian colonization in South America, and Northcote Parkinson, who says that "Portugal and Spain were more medieval than renaissance when their overseas adventure began. They were still living in a world of saints and knights errant, of monks and medieval castles." [5] The fact that the Spaniards and Portuguese were seized by a lust for gold and a thirst for commerical adventure did not make their efforts at conquest any less medieval.

Actually, the Europe of the Middle Ages had been experiencing materialistic ambitions for a long time. For example, the Crusades of the Middle Ages were not prompted solely by a mystic impulse to propagate the faith. Also at work was the materialistic impulse to conquer new sources of wealth and expand Christian commerce with the "infidels," the inhabitants of the mysterious East, who were thought to be fabulously rich. In general, the late Middle Ages was a period of mixture of interests and motivations, in Portugal as elsewhere, though the materialistic factor—which was eventually to produce capitalism as the dominant economic system—was to develop far more rapidly in some countries than in others, in Portugal with relative slowness. By the Age of Discovery, when most European countries had advanced beyond this Crusader outlook, the Spaniards and the Portuguese began the last of their Crusades (pursued this time by sea)—the conquest of South and Central America.

In the early sixteenth century the Portuguese were still backward in methods of trade, by no means as sophisticated as, for example, such a mercantilist people as the Dutch. Portuguese navigators and colonizers everywhere revealed their inexperience in what to them was a new métier. And the settlement of Northeast Brazil is a perfect demonstration of this backwardness. Portugal was ill prepared to make the most of the accidental discovery of Brazil. With only 1,000,000 inhabitants and with all the country's hopes turned toward profitable overseas conquests in Asia and Africa, Portugal had few human and material resources available for the colonization of such an immense territory as Brazil which was sparsely inhabited by wandering Stone Age tribes. In a short time, however, legends arose of marvelous riches to be found in this new country. These stories whetted the appetite of other European peoples on the march and encouraged them to dispute Portugal's possession of a South American treasure. Now Portugal decided to make the great effort which would be necessary to occupy and defend Brazil at all costs.

This was the situation in Portugal in 1534, a situation aggravated by internal pressures,[6] when King John III decided to convert the scattered settlements on the Brazilian coast into great feudal-type domains. His first step was to give the captaincy of Pernambuco to Duarte Coelho, veteran of the Indian campaigns. This huge land grant, which extended for sixty leagues (about two hundred fifty miles) along the coast, from the Iguarassu to the São Francisco River, was to be used to grow sugar cane.

As the capital of his great fief, Duarte Coelho founded the town of Olinda—built on top of a hill several miles from the harbor where the sugar was to be shipped back to Portugal. The very location of this capital is a clear indication (as Oliveira Lima, statesman, diplomat and historical essayist, has pointed out) of the commercial ineptitude of the Portuguese. They proposed to carry on a seaborne trade with Europe and the homeland. And yet they turned their backs on the harbor at the mouths of the Capiberibe and Beberibe rivers—whose fertile valleys were already cultivated with cane—and from the estuary from which sugar had been shipped to Lisbon since 1526. It was here, at these river mouths, that an almost complete world monopoly on sugar was to be concentrated for the next two centuries. Nevertheless, economic advantage was ignored. By climbing the slopes of Olinda to set up their medieval "burg," the Portuguese showed clearly that though they were greedy for wealth, they did not possess the Dutchman's gift for trade. The Dutch were soon to dominate world commerce; and following the sweet scent of sugar, they finally landed in Northeast Brazil at the beginning of the seventeenth century, established a colony and founded as its capital what is today the city of Recife. The Dutch capital, far from being perched on a hill, was originally located on an island at the mouth of the Capiberibe River, at the tip of the Olinda peninsula, and connected to the mainland by a bridge. Except for the Dutch intrusion it is possible that the city of Recife, today the port capital of the Nordeste, might never have existed. The difference between sea-connected Recife and Olinda on its hill is a good measure of the gap that separated the feudalistic Portuguese colonizers from the mercantilist Dutch.

As further proof of their limitations in trade, the Portuguese, having undertaken their ventures into the Indies expressly to eliminate the Arab middleman who sold the products of the East to Europe through Venice, soon found themselves performing the same secondary role. They sold their raw materials to other European peoples, who distributed them directly among centers of consumption and thereby far exceeded the Portuguese in profits. By maintaining a monopoly on refining sugar, Venice kept a third of the profits which would otherwise have gone to the Portuguese.

Oliveira Lima notes that "In matters of commerce the Peninsula [Spain and Portugal] never succeeded in developing a profitable system. At the height of its prosperity in the 16th century, Lisbon was no more than a point for transshipping overseas cargoes to Flanders. The homeland did not know how to create mercantile relations with other European nations."

It is evident too that at the time Brazil was being opened up, the feudal social structure of Portugal was beginning to show signs of disintegration. The absolute power of the agrarian aristocracy was waning, and the landlords who could escape from ruin in the countryside looked to the cities for new means of preserving their privileges. The rural aristocracy exchanged the power of noble birth for the power of money. But this is not to imply that the Portuguese followed the same course in Brazil as at home. Many historians, both in Brazil and abroad, have erred in translating Portuguese history into the Brazilian context. According to this point of view, Brazilian colonization, arising from a simultaneous expansion of maritime trade and the disintegration of the feudalistic Portuguese regime, followed the same lines of historic development as society in the homeland. The economy of colonial Brazil is described, therefore, as an incipient mercantilism, rather than the decadent feudal arrangement it actually was. By further extension, the nature of plantation agriculture is conceived as fundamentally capitalistic, rather then feudal.[7]

But this is a mere apologetic. The truth is, the mother country sent out its most regressive elements to exploit Brazil. Far from developing new ideas and ways of behavior in response to their new environment, as the English did in North America, they never relinquished their dismal medieval baggage.

History shows that in all colonization, not only that of Portugal, the mother country invariably attempts to transplant in the colonies the economic and political institutions which will most tend to perpetuate control by the homeland. And whenever the colonial enterprise shows an inclination to use more advanced economic methods, the mother country attempts to impose political and legal institutions that are even more backward and oppressive. When economic coercion alone fails to maintain control, other forms of coercion are brought into play, even if they are economically self-defeating.

Colonial Brazil is a prime example of this historical imperative. In spite of the fact that the mercantilists were an important influence in Brazilian colonization, they were not as strong a factor as their fellow merchants in the mother country. Unable to put their stamp on the Brazilian economy, they were subordinated to the transplanted feudal system. The evolution that was underway in Portuguese society found no projection in Brazil. The seignorial class, to whom the great captaincies were assigned, made a determined effort to turn back the wheel of history. The great adventure for the ruined nobility who left Portugal was to revive feudalistic patterns in the tropics in order to possess estates more vast than anything known before—with vassals and servants and serfs toiling to provide the great seignior with wealth and power.

However, this hope of literally resurrecting institutions that were on their way out in Portugal soon faded. There were no serfs available and native labor proved more and more unmanageable, but the "men of quality" from a debt-ridden and ruined nobility were not prepared to create a new model of the old world by the sweat of their brow. "These *fidalgos*," wrote Oliveira Viana, "come from a society still organized on a feudal model: the profession of arms alone is noble; it alone provides honor and status. They lack a feeling for the dignity of agricultural labor which was so deep among the Romans of the time of Cincinnatus."

What they really lacked most was money. As a result, colonization had to be carried on by a combination of impoverished noblemen and plebeians who had grown rich on trade and usury. There was only one condition—the "men of quality" had to stand above the "men of wealth." As I have noted earlier, all over the Iberian peninsula, but more deeply in Portugal than in Spain, the ideological trappings of medievalism were still very much in evidence. Sea trade, the main source of a rudimentary accumulation of capital, had created a small well-to-do middle class, but little of the power of the state had come into its hands, unlike the case in Northern Europe. Diogo de Gouveia, who inspired and formulated plans for Portuguese colonization in South America, definitely thought in terms of nobility, not of the bourgeoisie. "The best thing, sire," he advised King John

III in his letter of 1532, "is to give the land to your vassals."

The dominant position of "men of quality" in colonial Brazil is clearly shown in the caste spirit which governed the division of the vast new territories won from the Indians, particularly in the assignment of the best and largest shares. It was inevitable because the homeland itself was essentially feudalistic. Of course, it is true that by the sixteenth century the Portuguese economy had already advanced from a "natural" to a mercantilist stage, but this had taken place without any drastic adjustments in the social structure. The old pecking order still remained. And certain notable Brazilian historians and economists have erred in classifying the colonial regime as capitalistic.

The fact that in the sixteenth century there had been an extraordinary expansion of sea trade in Portugal, leading in turn to the growth of a mercantilist economy of some scope, led Roberto Simonsen to fall into this error. He introduced into Brazilian historiography a thesis that has influenced many Brazilian thinkers. "In reality," Simonsen writes, "Portugal in 1500 no longer lived under a feudal regime. With his navigation policy, his system of international monopolies, his economic maneuvers to supplant the Venice spice trade, King Manuel is an authentic capitalist." [8]

From there he proceeds to the following conclusion: "It does not seem reasonable to me that almost all Brazilian historians should so exaggerate the feudal aspect of the land grant system; some even go so far as to classify it as a backward step . . . Wishing to occupy and colonize the new land, and not have the resources for this purpose in the royal treasury, Portugal handed over large concessions for this purpose to the nobles or *fidalgos*, some of them rich landowners, others veterans of the expeditions to the Indies. From an economic point of view . . . it does not seem reasonable to me to liken this system to feudalism." Then, going even further, he says that in Portugal at the beginning of the sixteenth century feudalism was already extinct.

In my view, this eminent historian's arguments do not prove his thesis. He portrays Portugal as a society in which commerce, trade and the accumulation of capital had developed appreciably. Such factors did apply to some extent, but not to the point where it is justified to characterize the sixteenth-century Portuguese economy as capitalist. If the circulation of goods and money is the only criterion for classifying social systems, we have to put into that category all the societies that have been evolved by man since he emerged from primitive life. It would be impossible to distinguish among slave-based, feudal and capitalist systems, since all of these have a mercantilist aspect in greater or lesser degree.

What is basic to an economic regime is the system of production—the way men go about obtaining the means to live. This determines all other economic and social processes, including those by which marketable goods are distributed. In sixteenth-century Portugal agriculture was the principal source of production, although the money which the new mercantilist middle class amassed in their maritime ventures may even have exceeded the wealth of the landlords. True, a bourgeoisie was emerging with a powerful economic potential, and for more than a century this group had shared a little in the power of the state. But this new class was never strong enough to change the existing feudal system on the land. Land was a royal and noble monopoly. Since land was the main and most important means of production, the class which held unrestricted dominion over it could impose its will on other classes by economic and other means.

That's the way it has worked out in Brazil. The transplanted feudal monopolist system had to find novel solutions to new problems, but it kept the essential characteristics of the social structure that had served as its model. In fact, feudalism in Portugal had progressed one step ahead of its colonial counterpart, since it was based on serfdom rather than slavery. Moreover, the serf, encouraged by his relatively freer condition, had a higher production output. But in Brazil there were no serfs. Colonial feudalism had to retrogress to outright slavery to counterbalance the inefficiency of the slave system. It also had to take other steps that were backward compared with the tentative mercantilist development of the homeland economy; in effect, it reintroduced many practices typical of a "natural" economy. By way of compensation, there was a vast demand for sugar in the world market.

But none of the adaptations which the Brazilian environment forced on the colonial latifundium was able to dilute its overriding feudal character—a sort of compromise between slavery and serfdom. The slave provided for his own support by devoting a certain part of his time to fishing and hunting or to working the small garden plots set aside for his use. The slave-labor regime took on something of the character of the medieval system of paying in work or kind, together with other variants in the personal work relationship between slave and master. The colonial seigniors also made use of a mass of "free" tenants and hangers-on, who were employed in domestic service or other activities not directly connected with production.

In the plantation system, as through all sectors of the precapitalist economy of colonial Brazil, the fundamental element, to which all other economic relations were subordinated, was the feudal ownership of land as principal means of production. This was re-enforced by the Crown's monopoly on the sugar trade.

Why this insistence on the "feudalistic" character of Brazilian life? If the feudal character of the Brazilian plantation system is denied, if we were to assume, on the contrary, that the nature of the Brazilian economy and social posture was capitalist from the start, then no drastic change in Brazil's agrarian structure would be called for. Agrarian reform would be unnecessary in solving the current problems of the Northeast if the Brazilian agrarian structure has always had a "capitalist configuration." On the basis of this erroneous interpretation, an antireformist, antirevolutionary political strategy has been advanced—an evolutionist, gradualist concept of development according to which there is no need for basic reform. One need only add certain ingredients to the existing agrarian structure— more fertilizer, more mechanization, in a word, more capital—for agricultural progress to be widely accelerated. But obviously, such measures have not worked, and they will not.

Thus the theory of colonial capitalism is not the innocent historical proposition it first appears. It is a conservative, even reactionary, theory which fits perfectly into retrogressive political schemes. A denial, or even an underestimation, of the feudal content of the Brazilian plantation system would rob agrarian reform of its historical foundation and thwart it.

Agrarian reformers in modern Brazil aim to root out the feudal system which too often, and quite commonly in the Northeast, makes the sharecropper and the wage laborer in effect serfs. But their intention is not to organize the Brazilian peasants on collective farms in the Russian or Chinese style. What they propose is to promote, as far and as quickly as possible, the kind of freehold agriculture that exists in capitalist countries or, if not, a corporate type which is motivated not by speculative profit for the few but by the national good. As long as the feudal psychology prevails—viewing the great masses of Brazilian peasants as subhuman creatures—it is ultimately useless to try to shore up the rickety plantation system of the Northeast by stopgap supports.

Everything has been tried at one time or another— credit and technical assistance; concessions in exchange, and duty on capital equipment and processing and storage facilities; irrigation, flood control and drainage projects; economic missions to open up bigger markets abroad; price-fixing and market control schemes such as the coffee agreement. But all have failed and must fail again, since at bottom they are employed to preserve the status quo and the privileges of the few. The commonweal has never really been the object.

A quarter of all the people of Brazil live in the Northeast. Into their pockets goes only 10 per cent of the national income. That, in a nutshell, is the situation, and it is a monstrous abuse of the nation's human resources. Until these people are freed from the exploitation of speculative agriculture, permitted to raise fewer industrial crops for export and more for their own home use, taught how to plant hybrid corn instead of hiring out at serfs' wages to harvest cacao or raise absurdly scrawny cattle that take five years to fatten to marketable size, the situation is lost.

The fact has finally penetrated the Brazilian consciousness that the Northeast is paralyzed by an outmoded agricultural complex—obsolete in its human and economic relationships, sunk in ignorance and implacable greed. The most important of the relationships that must be destroyed is the colonial-feudal land monopoly with its concentration of ownership in the great estates. Even where familes have decayed and ancient ownerships fallen to corporations, the master-slave relation between the *patrão* and the *parceiro* persists. No permanent good can be achieved when a few fancy themselves lords of creation and beyond responsibility; they are capable of watching empty-eyed as thousands strain and die.

The very fact that land is still the fundamental production factor in Brazil indicates that an inferior economic concept which is in fact precapitalist still obtains. Agriculture in Brazil is not industrialized as it is in the United States. It has never been completely penetrated by capitalist ways of increasing production—mechanization, scientific techniques, efficient structures. In a fully developed capitalist agriculture these elements, rather than the land factor proper, contribute most to high productivity. The statistics of Brazilian agriculture—it cannot be emphasized

too strongly—clearly demonstrate that land as such, and
the simple ownership of it, still play the dominant role. By
extension, this monopolistic system of owning and using
land guarantees the landholding minority social and political as well as economic dominion.

In the 1600's the Jesuit father André João Antonil, also
known as João Antonio Andreoni, wrote *Cultura e Opulência do Brasil por suas Drogas e Minas* (*Culture and Wealth
of Brazil: Its Culture and Mines*). Antonil said: "It seems
that anyone who gets to be a seignior would like everybody
else to be a serf." [9] And in the nineteenth century Koster
noted "the great power and authority of the landowner not
only over his slaves, but over free persons of the poorer
classes." [10] Before the 1930's this same spirit took on the
form of *coronelismo* (political and economic bossism), and
with some slight changes in style, it has retained that form
to this day. In sum, feudalism survives and Brazil suffers
from it.

chapter 4

COLONIAL BRAZIL: PROGRESS DENIED

Wₕₐₜ do we mean by "absence of a people"?

We mean that only belatedly has a popular consciousness emerged in Brazil. Throughout most of the four and a
half centuries of Brazilian history the masses remained totally unaware of themselves as a group, blankly ignorant of
their size and of the strength inherent in their number—
their horizons were bounded by the few square miles in
which they lived out their brief lives.

The ability of the Brazilian to develop as a social animal (as the French peasant did in breaking out of the feudal mold during the Revolution) was systematically ham-
pered by the feudal relationships that existed between the

leaders and the led and between the peasants and the land. For generation after generation the great majority of the population had no political significance, no voice, nor even any social consciousness. The mass drifted through life, leaving not a trace behind. And the least sign of emergence was crushed or smothered. There was change, but it was worked by the will of the elite. All the important events of Brazilian history were the work of a few: the separation from the motherland, the organization of newly sprung states into a republic, even the framing of the immensely long and detailed Brazilian Constitution—a document so rich in compromise that it could not possibly threaten the various forms of privilege which it represented.

In sum, the history of Brazil in one critical sense—that is, in the obdurate insistence on preserving its feudalistic heritage—has been a struggle against progress. It was so in the days of King John III, and it was no less so in the apparently more liberal days of the Marquês de Pombal. Pombal is remembered for having abolished the captaincies in 1775. Far more important, he also expelled the Jesuits from Brazil, thus smashing the educational system, however feeble, and scoring another victory for the Stone Age. Nor was it actually much different in the days of Dom Pedro, under whose aegis the Portuguese garrisons were driven out and independence was made the vogue. Revolution meant only the fragmentation of the power structure into new regional and local clots; it did not touch the people deeply. No peasant Spartacus arose from their midst, nor could he, since there was no people as a collective entity— the Brazilian mass was a mere aggregation. So there has been through the centuries the same melancholy struggle against progress, the same denial of the human spirit, now intense, now momentarily relaxed.

At the time that Portugal began to give serious thought to settling and developing the new colony of Brazil, the sympathies of the Crown were divided between "men of quality" and "men of wealth," and the latter were preferable, in the royal view, as future colonizers. However, they were not to prevail.

In Portugal at this period a struggle was going on between the run-down seignorial class—holders of broad feudal powers, favored by the Church, standard-bearers of the medieval tradition—and a nascent bourgeoisie which had many interests in common with the Crown. In this conflict, characteristic of the sixteenth century, we find an explanation for many otherwise obscure aspects of Brazilian history. The interests of the two classes were opposed, and contradictions resulting from this opposition—on the one hand, the Crown's concessions to the nobles, often made under Church instigation and sponsorship, and on the other, victories won by the merchants at the nobles' expense—carried over into the Brazilian colony.

Although at the end of the fifteenth century, feudalism in Portugal still maintained its despotic rule virtually unchecked, a cosmopolitan mercantile class had begun to emerge by the middle of the next century. These rich and influential people had values and interests which rivaled those of feudal barons. From this point forward the conflict between the decadent world of feudalism and the new bourgeois world sharpened.

It would have been in the merchants' interest to simply extract raw materials from the colonies and traffic in slaves,

as in Africa. However, the feudalistic Portuguese nobles regarded Brazil as a colossal opportunity to recoup their
agricultural fortunes, and the Crown wanted to use its royal
land grants, or captaincies, to salvage the deteriorating Portuguese agriculture. At home the feudal economy was in
decline; the fields were being abandoned as the population
moved to the towns and cities. To reverse this trend, the
Crown had promulgated decrees governing land tenure
which prescribed penalties for proprietors who failed to
keep their lands under cultivation. If they did not begin
producing again within a certain time after a warning—six
months, a year, two years—their lands were expropriated
and given to those who would cultivate them. This was only
a cautious revision of traditional feudal tenure. Even so, it
was obviously difficult to put into practice.

It is clear that the agricultural situation in sixteenth-
century Portugal must have been relatively serious and the
misery and depopulation of the rural areas relatively advanced to justify the strong measures that appear in the
charters and ordinances of the period. These severe and in-
soluble domestic agricultural problems explain why the
Crown was not itself interested in tilling still more lands
overseas. And these were tracts so huge that their very size
fascinated the *fidalgos*. As for the *nouveau riche* merchants,
they were already sophisticated enough to realize that speculation in overseas agriculture would be risky.

But at this juncture a miraculous product came into
view that was to change the whole course of Portuguese history. The product was sugar. The rich black soil of the
Northeast coastal strip of Brazil proved to be ideal for
growing sugar cane. As for the techniques of cultivation,

one could draw upon the experience of growers from the island of Madeira. Cane was highly profitable, and prices were going up. However, it would be necessary to violate a sacrosanct colonizing principle and install processing plants in the colony, rather than, as usual, in the mother country, since the raw material could not be transported long distances across the sea. The juices had to be extracted on the spot; otherwise the cane would dry up and be lost. Also, it seemed that in this case the homeland really had little to fear from such an arrangement. So far in Portugal, the marriage of mill to agriculture had been characterized by the subordination of the mill, and it could be assumed that this subordination would be the rule in the colony as well. In practice, this gave the *fidalgo* landowner the final say and meant that the new industry need not be feared as a liberating and enlightening force that would be dangerous to the Crown.

Sugar was to be a great boon to the home establishment. It could be produced in a way that permitted Portugal to solve its basic domestic problems and overcome its own economic dualism. Sugar would make it possible to settle the new lands in a manner that suited the feudal mentality. At the same time the guarantee of big profits would attract the merchants, giving them an opportunity to be middlemen and bankers to the nobles, who would be basically entrusted with the sugar-growing enterprise.

Precious metals were pouring into Europe in increasing quantities; trade and markets were expanding, prices were continuing to rise and the sale of all consumer goods, particularly sugar, was growing by leaps and bounds. The demand for sugar would be enormous, and Portuguese shipping would also benefit. Sugar was indeed a miracle product, destined to be the great staple of international commerce for almost a century.

The Northeast Brazil sugar-growing enterprise which sprang up now, in these early colonial days, in turn determined the land-tenure system and the kind of society that it generated. The sugar-plantation system was perhaps unique in history insofar as it brought together three elements rarely seen in concert: feudalistic land tenure, slave labor, and capitalistic investment and trading practices. In sugar cane the *sesmaria*, or royal-land-grant, system found its economic destiny.

It was Martim Afonso de Souza, on whom the Crown had conferred sweeping powers, who laid the foundations of a new economic policy in the undeveloped colony, a policy based solidly on two institutions—the land grant and the sugar mill. The *sesmaria*, or secondary land grant by the royal concessionaire, and the *engenho*, or sugar mill where the cane was pressed, were to be the pillars of colonial Brazil.

Thus the colony of Vera Cruz entered a more advanced stage of land use. The few scattered trading settlements established during the purely extractive stage, "factories" where brazilwood was collected for its dye content, had produced no great result. The old hit-or-miss extractive enterprises, over which it was impossible to exercise even a minimum of fiscal and administrative control, henceforth would be replaced by a settled and organized form of production which would be much easier to tax and control from home. This agrarian scheme left an indelible mark on Brazilian history.

Rapidly the seeds sown by the Crown began to germi-
nate. "When King John III systematically divided our territory into latifundia called captaincies, military officers
called captains-general were already there, appointed for
the captaincies of Brazil. What was then done was to divide
up the land, and assign and proclaim to the colonists their
respective rights and duties, and the rights, charters, trib-
utes and things that the colonists had to accord to the King
and his donees [*donatários*], each of whom was issued the
charter of his grant [*donatária*], with the sum of his charter powers. This charter was a kind of contract, whereby the
sesmeiros, or colonists, became perpetual tributaries of the
Crown, also of their donors, or captains-general. Land divided into seignorial holdings within a seignorial state—
such is the general outline of the administrative system during the first phase of our history." [1]

In this way both property and state were set up overseas
according to the homeland's feudal ground rules. Vast
reaches of territory were handed over to masters endowed
by the Crown with absolute authority over everything in
sight, including people. In this hierarchic system the original captaincies were divided into massive holdings and
given to great landowners, who had everything their own
way, in part because they were so far out of the Crown's
reach, in part through sheer force of arms. And since it was
not only noble birth, but money too, which determined how
much land the colonist would recieve from the royal donee,
both elements—land ownership and wealth—were marks
of the newly sprung rural aristocracy. The Crown's aim was
to hand over a monopoly on land to the nobility, to enfeoff
them in pure feudal tradition and at the same time to enlist

in the enterprise "men of means," the favorite sons of the bourgeois class grown rich in trade.

Not surprisingly, therefore, along with the power which was originally concentrated in the hands of Martim Afonso went a triple misson: to make grants of land called *sesmarias*, to develop these grants into plantations and to construct sugar mills. The *alcaide-mor*, or Lord Protector of the House of Braganza, carried out these goals with shrewdness and foresight. He even found ways to persuade Flemish and German bankers to finance some of the Brazilian sugar mills. And after the departure of Martim Afonso the scheme was advanced no less shrewdly by Duarte Coelho, the *donatário*, or royal donee, of Pernambuco, who recounts his industrious efforts in his correspondence with the king: "I gave orders to build sugar mills, the trusses for which I brought pre-cut from Portugal," and "we will soon finish a very large and perfect mill and I am giving orders to start others," he wrote in a letter dated April 27, 1542.[2] In another letter, dated April 14, 1549, he referred to a mill "of my making" and mentioned again that he was founding others, "which is a fine thing and greatly enhances the good of the land." [3]

Fifteen years after Martim Afonso received his three royal charters, the building of sugar mills was still the colonizers' main preoccupation, as one can see from Duarte Coelho's same letter of 1549: "Among all the inhabitants and founders of the colony some build sugar mills because they have the means to do this, others plant cane and others cotton and others food crops, which is the principal and most necessary thing for the land . . . others are masters of mills and others master sugar makers, carpenters, blacksmiths, potters and craftsmen of forms and bells for the mills . . . and I send for them from Portugal and Galicia and the Canaries at my own cost and some of those who come here to build sugar mills bring them."

Obviously, turning the *sesmarias* into sugar factories was not the only colonial activity. However, through the centuries the growing of crops for food—though Duarte Coelho may have recognized it *pro forma* as a "principal and necessary activity"—continued to be subordinated to the growing of sugar cane.

About ninety years later, in 1639, when the Dutch took over the Northeast of Brazil, van der Dussen, struggling with the food shortage, complained in a report to the Chamber of Nineteen of the West India Company in Amsterdam: "Thus you should always keep the warehouses well filled with food and not count on the products of the region, not even on food supplies that traders or private individuals send there, because these are almost all consumed at the mills and sold in the interior. The result is, when trouble comes and you think of getting something from the merchants, everything is empty, as happened with us in the hard times we have just gone through."

This was the picture during the whole colonial period. The enfeoffed land absorbed all human energy exclusively in the interest of colonial or absentee landlords, whose purpose, of course, was to squeeze out as much income in money and tribute as possible. Little if any attention was given to the needs of the workers, who had no share in the profits and nothing to offer but their labor.

There were laws, but they were impotent whenever they countered the landlords' interests. "The trivial plantings of manioc," as Rodrigues de Brito described them in 1807, "which grows on any kind of land," was not an appropriate use for the "rare and precious fields of *massapê,* to which Nature has awarded the privilege of producing first-class sugar." [4]

And since not only the fields covered with this very rich soil, but all land whatsoever near the consuming centers, belonged to the great landlords, where were subsistence crops to find a place? The fact is, from the very beginning the plantation and the sugar mill were an implacable deterrent to a subsistence agriculture.

Judging from what Duarte Coelho confesses in one of his letters of 1549, the economic and political power of the landlords was sky high at this time: "I would rather go against the people than against the owners of the sugar mills." Meanwhile, beginning in the period when Tomê de Souza headed the colonial government, events occurred which were of the greatest importance for the evolution of the Brazilian economy—events which sealed a division between the completely feudal North and the less feudal, more bourgeois South.

"To Bahia and Pernambuco," notes Felisberto Freire,[5] "flowed by preference those who wanted to draw profits from the land through slaves and sharecroppers. The owner of the land, who lived in the capital [Bahia] and enjoyed the benefits of the Court, had someone else fell the forests and work his lands for him. But in Rio, São Paulo and Espírito Santo, particularly in the 16th century, it was the farmer himself, side by side with his slave, who did the agricultural work."

In *História Territorial,* Freire describes the character

of the class which presided over the sharing out of land from the first century of the colonial period: "The grants to the North were generally larger than those in the South. With the exception of the royal land grant of Visconde de Asseca in Campos, the *sesmarias,* or grants by royal donees, in the South were not more than three leagues [about twelve miles] in breadth, wheras in the North we find grants of 20 and 30 leagues or more. The grants to Garcia d'Avila and his relatives, for example, extended from Bahia to Piauí a distance of 200 leagues [about 800 miles]."

The explanation for this tremendous difference in the size and quality of the land grants was, as Felisberto Freire writes: "The reason for this lies in the differing social status of the colonists who came to Brazil . . . This difference . . . put obstacles in the way of settlement in the North, the main one being the extensive land grants. Thus, a man of the people had to be either a simple tenant on the land, or to move out into the *sertão* region, which was full of Indians and other difficulties beyond the power of the poor to overcome."

Before the end of the sixteenth century a whole class of absentee owners were living parasitically on the land, divorced from actual production and indifferent to social need. "In general the concessionaires were the nobility from the capital of the captaincy, many of them officers and representatives of the government itself. Such were Alvaro da Costa, Tomê de Souza, Miguel de Moura and many others, all of whose *sesmarias* [secondary grants] were veritable *donatários* [primary royal grants]. The system of renting to the small colonists then began. Now we have the agent of Dom Alvaro subdividing his grant among the colonists, so creating a class of tenant farmers contributing much to the owner's prosperity. It was precisely this class that was the first form of free labor in Brazil, side by side with slave labor . . ."

The Ordinances of the Kingdom had decreed that the size of each land grant should be limited by the capacity of the grantee to put the land to use, so that "no more land should be given to one person than it may reasonably seem he can make use of." But in practice this broke down. The regime of Tomê de Souza had the effect of officially ratifying—and not of introducing, as Cirne Lima states[6]—the "latifundian spirit" which was to guide the distribution of land. For the powerful, those with nobility or wealth, there were no limits to the grants except those imposed by the Indians who were resisting expropriation by the armed Portuguese intruders. The Crown smiled on applicants who had enough resources to set up adequate fortifications and defenses to pacify the whole vast region. Actually, these people had to make only a token effort to work their enormous grants.

Under this endowment system the decisive factor in qualifying was the social status of the concessionaire. Social status alone accounted for the unequal shares meted out to candidates. However, the smallest *sesmarias* were immense domains compared to what a single colonizer, or even a family, was actually capable of putting to agricultural use. Meanwhile, no small lots were handed out to people from the lower class, which might have raised them to yeomen. In this highly inequitable system, which distributed land only to the nobility and well-to-do gentry, the common man did not enter into the consideration. The land-less masses were viewed like the oxen at the mills, as two-legged animals to be yoked to the heavy feudal cart. They were marginal and faceless, denied the least means of access to the rights and privileges of their overlords.

Whatever decrees were issued by the Crown to restrict the size of territories were merely a perfunctory response to persistent abuse of privilege and to the endless lawsuits over land in which the more powerful nobles always came out the winners, with resulting prejudice to the colonization process. Among various royal decrees regulating the size of the *sesmarias* was that of December 27, 1695. This decree declared that no resident should be granted an area more than four leagues in length and one league in width (an old Brazilian league was about 4.09 miles): "which is what each colonist may comfortably populate." Or so the decree is recorded in a manuscript attributed to the Marquês de Aguiar.[7] It is easy to imagine the difficulty of enforcing such restrictions whose purpose was to increase production and taxes.

The Brazilian mercantile system, attempting to improve on the natural economy, did indeed set in motion a trend toward the division of labor. But this trend became abortive when the landlords subdivided their domains among individual farmers and then appropriated the farmers' profits as rent, while they themselves remained apart from the actual production process. In this way they got around the basic purpose of the land-grant decrees, which in theory imposed on beneficiaries the obligation to cultivate and care for their lands themselves. So much of the land was rented out that the anticipated revenue to the Crown did not materialize; and so the Royal Decree of 1695 was issued to remedy the situation. The decree created "aside from the obligation to pay a tenth to the Order of Christ, and the other customary obligations, a land rent or tax, according to the size and fertility of the lands in question." There is nothing to show, however, that this tax was enforced before 1777, when Manoel de Cunha e Menezes, governor of Bahia, began to collect a land tax on each new *sesmaria*. In the eighteenth century the privileged nature of land owner-ship became even more pronounced. As the colony spread in town and countryside the control of the land monopolists was strengthened still further, while the disadvantaged sec-tors of the population were falling into ever greater difficul-ties. Meanwhile, there was severe administrative disorder (see the trenchant description by Caio Prado, Jr.).[8]

The Crown had to make a choice between the two camps into which the colony had split, and it was in keeping with the royal interest to side with the powerful landlords and affirm their privileges. Under the economic and political conditions existing in eighteenth-century Portugal, it could hardly have been otherwise. Class antagonisms in colonial Brazil went hand in hand with similar conflicts within the crumbling homeland.

"On the one hand were the landowning Brazilians, who considered themselves the nobility, brought up to an expan-sive and free-spending way of life, disdaining work and thrift; on the other hand was the *mascate* [literally "ped-dler," but meaning johnny-come-lately Portuguese who had made money in the towns], the immigrant grown rich, trained in a rough school of work and parsimony, who, with his money, had begun to throw the nobles into the shade.

Opposition to the Portuguese immigrant businessman— *mascate*, "sailor," "leadfoot" or whatever the epithet used to describe him, became widespread, because he, the outsider, was grabbing up all trade in the colony, wholesale and retail, and keeping the Brazilian out. The Brazilian-born colonist was finding it harder and harder to get along. So the conflict spread and deepened. It was this economically grounded hatred that led to the so-called Guerra dos Mascates, or "Peddlers' War," 1710–11. Strife broke out when old-fashioned Olinda on its medieval hill, the political capital of Pernambuco, became jealous and embittered about the raising of commercial-minded Recife to town status. Recife, of course, prevailed, kept its municipal privileges and eventually supplanted Olinda as the Pernambucan capital.

What was happening in Brazil at this time was only one instance of a general spread of bourgeois economy through all the Western world in the eighteenth century. In Brazil, as elsewhere, the landowners fell in debt to the merchants, particularly after the periodic crises in the international sugar market. Meanwhile, the Crown was greedily reaching out for more taxes, seeking by means of the royal "tenth" and other imposts to pay for its excesses. Yet the effort to despoil the colony was directed less at the landholders than at other economic groups; for the Brazilian rural aristocracy, with few exceptions, constituted a supporting faction for the Crown in its policy of drastically restricting the development of manufactures in the colonies, to the detriment, it was thought, of similar enterprises in the homeland. And as the mother country strengthened its stranglehold on trade and manufacturing, the colonial concentration of the basic means of production, the land, in the hands of a few was likewise strengthened.

The discovery of gold and diamonds in the early 1700's led to a rash of mining ventures that for a while were to dominate the life of the colony. This mining fever had a disastrous effect on agriculture and bred lasting conflicts. But the grip of the landowners remained unshaken. On the contrary, while farming activity was generally declining and farmers were becoming impoverished and the fields were being abandoned, a powerful minority found ways to surmount the difficulties, make the most of a distressed situation and become still richer.

When the mining fever had run its course, the colony found itself in desperate straits, made worse by the land monopoly. Fields lay fallow, and an enormous mass of unemployed were prevented from working them because of the legal obstacles to owning small- and medium-sized properties. The feudalistic land-grant laws were incapable of serving the very purpose for which ostensibly they had been created; that is, to expand use of the land and populate the country.

To get clear title to a *sesmaria*, three conditions had to be met: first, the land had to be surveyed; second, its features had to be described; third, there must be a commitment to cultivate it. The first condition was rarely met. There were few available surveyors, and it would have cost a fortune to map hundreds of square miles. The other two conditions were honored more often in the breach than in the observance. As a rule, land-grant charters were issued on the basis of inaccurate, and in some cases deliberately falsified, information supplied by the applicant and never checked. Sometimes, for lack of clearly located bounds and base points, the same piece of land was given to two or more parties. The absence of clear, legally recorded boundaries greatly facilitated land grabbers in absorbing the property of small, defenseless owners. Even to this day the practice of claim jumping continues and is responsible for bloody family feuds. The boundary lines of one big estate, as recorded on a map hanging on the wall, were as follows: "Bounded on the north by the Taquari River, although it is a long way off; on the south by where you can see the mountains; on the east by a lake that sometimes goes dry; on the west by God only knows." Moreover, unused lands reverted to the state, which made them again available for disposal.

Beginning in 1780 land charters prohibited the subdivision of land and thereby held back small-scale landholding for many, many years, at the same time perpetuating the plantation system and the great estates, along with one-crop agriculture and the slave-labor system. In fact, the whole economy of the Brazilian Northeast rested on these three institutions until the end of the nineteenth century. During the Dutch occupation John Maurice of Nassau had obliged millowners to cultivate manioc and distribute land among the poorer colonists, with the promise to buy whatever they produced. But this passing reform made no lasting impression on Brazilian monoculture. The unaided labor of small farmers was incapable of opening up such a vast virgin territory, while the large-scale tropical agriculture, primitive as it was, continued to show huge profits. Thus from the beginning the cards were stacked against the bourgeois, democratic type of land tenure that was established, at least as an ideal, in the settlement of North America. Building a sugar mill cost at least 300,000 cruzeiros and the labor of 150 to 200 workers. This automatically excluded the mass of people, however industrious they may have been. And there was no market for small, independent produce farmers, particularly since the large plantations were practically self-sufficient with regard to food. As a further deterrent, only the large estates had the means to defend themselves against Indian attacks; and finally, the planters were protected by a law which prohibited the making of spirits from cane in small stills and the growing of cotton on a limited scale.

The Resolution of July 17, 1822, abolished the land-grant system in Brazil, in tacit recognition of an untenable situation that threatened to become a real menace to the landlords. Rural masses in increasing numbers were flooding onto uncultivated private or public lands. It was these waves of squatters—or intruders, as they were called—that hastened the downfall of the land-grant institution. And now the authorities of colonial Brazil had to find some other means of preserving the feudally rooted estate.

Meanwhile, the squatters ushered in a new phase in Brazilian agrarian life. The squatters' struggle for land engendered a new capitalist, peasant form of ownership. And the development of cattle raising began a period in which the *sesmaria* evolved into a new type of large-scale property: the *fazenda*.

The first land grants to encourage the penetration and settlement of the hinterland of Bahia and the basins of its more important rivers were issued in the second half of the sixteenth century, after an outpost of the colonial government had been established in that area. The injunction "to introduce cattle within six months" or within six months "to start a *fazenda*"—stipulated on almost all deeds of the period—was meant to clarify the Crown's colonial objectives: the strip along the Northeast coast, particularly the best and most accessible land, was to be reserved for sugar cane, while the interior was to be given over to cattle, thus providing a second avenue for settlement. At first the term *fazenda* was limited to cattle ranches (*estâncias* in Southern Brazil), but later it came to mean any kind of large agricultural enterprise; for example, a coffee *fazenda*. Although the *engenho*, or sugar mill and plantation, and *fazenda* had a common origin, it was not long before unforeseen events forced these two types of latifundia to take divergent courses.

The colonial nobility remained concentrated in the sugar plantations, a bulwark against the infiltration of "plebian" ownership. There for a long time the homeland would find its main colonial support and its most complete collaboration. Traders and moneylenders were also oriented in favor of the sugar planters, who provided markets for the slave trade, an opportunity for usury and the only really significant outlet for European knickknacks and luxury goods. In this respect the more remote *fazendas* represented from the very start, continuing on at least until the nineteenth century, something of a break with the medieval and slaveholding heritage of the sugar plantations.

The *engenho* combined agricultural and cane-processing activities and was largely worked by African slaves. In addition, some paid freemen were employed in the crafts, anticipating in a minor way a "capitalist" system of production. It was a strange economic situation in which free-men tended to regress to serfdom and serfs to slavery, while successful merchants became aristocrats with titles, and nobles straight out of feudalism were transformed into slave-owners.

In the *engenho* the owner was absolute master. To be a *senhor de engenho,* says Antonil, "is a title to which many aspire, since it carries with it the status whereby one is served, obeyed and respected by many." Throughout the history of the sugar-plantation system, properties almost always belonged to one man and were handed down to his heirs. The tendency toward association and combination, so strongly evident elsewhere in sixteenth-century mercantilism, was unknown in rural Brazil. The plantation was a family-held fief and could not admit any form of partnership that might threaten the family's continuity of possession. The lord of the sugar plantation considered himself a miniature king with an inalienable right to his lands. The feudal absoluteness of his outlook distinguished him from the *fazendeiro,* the other kind of large-propertied man, who started out raising cattle and later turned to coffee and other products. On the *fazenda* there was a kind of free-labor system at least remotely capable of capitalist development. However, sharecroppers and field hands who are only nominally free are a long way from being yeomen.

The sugar economy obstinately limited social life to the scattered rural centers. As in medieval times, in sixteenth-century Brazil it was the country, through the sugar planters, which ruled the towns. Only very slowly did the towns grow into centers of commerce, banking and trade. As time went on, the landowners often had to turn to the bankers, mortgaging their property to borrow needed cash. This gave rise to great antagonisms, and it explains many of the insurrections that stud Brazilian history. Often the debt-harassed landlords allied with the discontented masses against the businessmen and moneylenders of only recent Portuguese extraction.

In sum, the sugar latifundium had to struggle almost unceasingly to survive. From the start, the *engenho* was organized as an armed camp, a feudal fortress capable of beating off Indians seeking to recover their lands. Later, raids mounted from runaway slave settlements and foreign invasions gave the planters additional opportunities to exercise their strength as men of arms. Sometimes their struggles coincided with legitimate national interests and popular aspirations. Here we come face to face with one of the contradictory aspects of the sugar-cane latifundium. In some instances its efforts to stay alive and perpetuate itself, which as a rule follow impulses contrary to a democratic evolution, have combined with the defense of patriotic and progressive principles. But it was primarily rural feudalism that the planters were defending, even when this placed them in paradoxical positions—for example, when they resisted and overcame invaders of notably bourgeois and urban tendency, such as the Dutch, or when they fought against intrusive traders and moneylenders who were monopolizing the commerce of cities and towns, this on behalf and behest of the mercantile interests of the Portuguese metropolis. Too often the Brazilian national motto, "Order and Progress," has been in practice "Order Against Progress."

The Brazilian "corral" was originally a simple adjunct to the sugar mill. Oxen were bred there to pull the heavy plantation carts and supply power, in teams of a dozen or more, for the primitive presses where juice was squeezed from the cane. The cattle raised in the plantation corral were used almost exclusively as work animals. The ox was as indispensable as the Negro slave, and many writers report that on average-sized plantations there were as many oxen as slaves; however, the animals were exhausted so fast they had to be replaced every three years. The slaves, on the other hand, lasted longer. In time, as the demand for sugar continued to grow, the corrals of the *engenhos* were unable to keep up. This must have been the main reason for the gradual separation of *engenho* and *fazenda*, with the latter, meanwhile, forced to move into the backlands to find grazing room. This invasion of the *sertão* was not accomplished without repeated clashes between ranchers and farmers. A royal decree at the beginning of the sixteenth century ordered the cattle-raising area to be kept at least more than ten leagues (about forty miles) from the coast. However, by 1701, when a decree set legal limits to large-scale ranching, the heavy demand for work animals, the gradual increase in meat consumption and above all the discovery of new uses for cowhides had already provided a conclusive stimulus to the expansion of cattle raising, to its separation from farming and its migration deep into the interior.

Cattle ranching was an enormously important factor in the formation of the Brazilian economy and society as a whole. It caused frontiers to be pushed back at an accelerated pace, and it led to a more permanent settlement of the land than did the search for precious metals and for Indians to enslave.

The seventeenth century, when stock raising began in earnest, also witnessed the start of tobacco raising, which created an additional demand for leather, to be used in wrapping tobacco leaves. According to Antonil, in the succeeding century Bahia alone exported 25,000 leather-covered bales of tobacco in a single year. Leather for shoes was also exported to Lisbon, after the hides from the ranches had been tanned in the cities. Ranching was thus set apart from the sugar-based economy; agriculture was separate from manufacturing, stock raising from tanning, city from countryside.

The development of ranching was in Portugal's best interests because it fitted nicely into the Brazilian export trade. The influence of a domestic Brazilian market for beef seems to have been of only secondary importance in the encouragement of this new form of land use. Antonil reports that a hide with the hair still on was worth 2,100 *reis* and the carcass as meat was worth 4,000 *reis,* or only slightly less than twice as much. Somewhat later the chroniclers report that in some cases cattle were used only for their hides and the meat was thrown away.

The tradition of rural Brazil derived mainly from the *engenho* rather than the *fazenda.* Ranching in the backlands, on the other hand, was correlated with the growth of cities on the coast. Urban activities had little support from the sugar plantations, by which, in fact, they were historically opposed. But the ranching interests were tied to the urban markets and came to a focus in that mainspring of the towns, the cattle fair.

From the earliest times the cowmen were drawn to the endless open range of the interior, a space too vast for any individual control. Ranching had to be pursued collectively, and the *fazenda*, earlier than any other latifundian enterprise in Brazil, developed a system of renting out land. This came about despite the fact that the ranch was in many respects similar to the plantation and preserved much of the common feudal heritage. Inevitably men of only limited resource were allowed first to rent and later even to share in the ownership of land. In this way the *fazenda* stood in opposition to the *engenho* and was a force tending to undermine the absolute privileges of the colonial nobility.

The nature of work on the ranches, the absence of a proprietor, the impossibility of superintending the work directly, the smaller number of workers—in short, the whole system of cattle raising—was incompatible with slave labor. It required instead a somewhat modified form of servitude, even wage labor. Indian labor was used much more widely on the cattle ranches—which, incidentally, refutes the idea still held by certain official historians that they had no capacity for work. On the whole, as compared with the *engenho*, the *fazenda* was slightly more democratically inclined and represented a step forward. In one sense, of course, it might be considered more feudalist than the plantation, for its main beneficiaries were absentee owners who the sugar plantations, by which, in fact, they were historialso made the cattle-ranch system more vulnerable to fragmentation. The cowhand of the backlands was always a much freer man, like the craftsman of the towns, than the workers on the sugar plantations. In *Economic History*, Roberto Simonsen describes the cattle ranch as having "a typically local character, tending to produce free men with capital of their own."

There were three main ways of getting to own or operate a ranch: (1) by renting, though at first this arrangement was illegal because the original owners of the land had no right to subdivide their concession; (2) by purchase, limited to the minority with ready cash; (3) by grant or *sesmaria*, which involved large acreages and was the perquisite of nobles and royal favorites; or (4) by handout, given to successful Indian fighters and slavers and to those who had rendered valuable military service to the Crown.

It was only later, after the land-grant system had ended, that the settlement of the hinterland became less restricted, allowing large-scale involvement by people of more modest means. Many of these people never got beyond the stage of squatter, living on small ranches or farms rather than building a *fazenda*. Their land was called *sítio* (mere site); and it was these *sítios* which paved the way for small-scale land ownership in general.

The great difference in the colonization of North and South Brazil (arising from the different social status of the colonists in the two regions) is of paramount importance in understanding Brazilian economic development. The people of lesser means and station tended to settle in the South in what is now São Paulo, while the more wealthy newcomers from Portugal converged on Bahia and Pernambuco in the North, where the best cane lands were located. The Portuguese caste system, more than climate, geography or racial considerations, best explains the economic supremacy of the Northeast during the first centuries, when land owner-ship was the decisive economic factor. It also explains the subsequent economic decline of the Northeast and the grow-ing dynamism of the South as the planter class and their descendants redoubled their efforts to preserve a hopelessly anachronistic way of life. The South became capitalistic, so to speak, as a matter of course. But the feudal Northeast re-sisted this natural development, opposed new settlements and refused to develop new markets or expand old ones. Obdurately cutting off its nose to spite its face, the North-east through the centuries sank ever deeper into its regres-sive mire.

From early days the land monopoly in the South was generally less despotic. A man could function better there and get ahead more easily. Rather than living parasitically on his rents, the South Brazilian landowner more often lived on his land and took charge of things himself. As a result, in the South land was subdivided earlier, soil was better used, immigrants settled more freely, new markets arose more quickly—all of which meant less feudal drag and a stronger potential for democracy. Therefore, it was in South and Central Brazil that a true industrial economy came into being first.

By the nineteenth century the hegemony over cattle pro-duction was no longer in the hands of the Northeast back-lander. The cattle ranchers of the South and Central Brazil-ian states of Minas Gerais, São Paulo, Mato Grosso and Goiás and the *estâncias* of Rio Grande do Sul were now in the lead—for which there were many reasons. Cattle raised on the hot, dry scrublands of the Northeast *sertão* were typically poorer than those of the South, and the Northern stockman had more difficulty paying his rents. Incapable of supervising his properties, the Northern absentee owner suffered from chronically inefficient management. His markets were far away and the people in them were poor, which lowered the price a herd could command. Stock-raising methods in the North were always more backward than in Central and South Brazil, where the owner was quite often the operator as well. Milk and its by-products were little valued in the North, and the *sertão*, moreover, had no land suitable for subsistence agriculture; neither corn nor forage was grown there, in contrast to the Central and Southern ranches.

But the decisive factor in the superiority of the South was its gradual development of a domestic market within reach of the ranches, which made it possible to sell cattle for meat as well as for hides. First the gold rush and later a wider distribution of land provided the stockmen of Minas Gerais, São Paulo and Rio Grande do Sul with an edge over the Northeast. In the North and the Northeast the only possible market for meat was the plantations, but these usually had their own herds. The sugar latifundium invariably had a pernicious effect on whatever was going on around it.

As we analyze social evolution in the Northeast, we are forced to conclude that at all stages of colonial history the feudal economic system was an enemy of real progress. The tinsel splendors of the Northeast during the seventeenth and part of the eighteenth centuries were only a surface phenomenon; and even so, they were limited to the ruling oligarchy. The great mass of people, as a marginal factor in the plantation economy, were left untouched by luxury and cultural splendor.

Like all colonial powers, Portugal used the Brazilian oligarchs to the Crown's advantage. The economist Gunnar Myrdal[9] graphically describes the fundamental difference between true economic development, which must benefit large sectors of the population, and the spurious colonial types, in which the masses have no share and no possibility of access. In the economy of the colonial Northeast only the dominant minority prospered and progressed, while the masses were always left outside looking in, a mere reservoir of manpower. And the gap between the elite and the oppressed became still more unbridgeable because of the continuing absence of a middle class, whose emergence was prevented by the lack of social mobility.

In sum, there was no social interplay, none of that sedimentation process by which a mass becomes a people, an entity claiming the allegiance of all social groups and classes, a living force that gives political meaning and direction to the historical thrust toward nationhood. It is this deficiency that explains in Brazilian history the almost complete absence of any total revolution which might have put an end to the colonial episode.

Resentment, humiliation and the burning urge to revolt against oppression never found a way to pass from the level of suppressed antagonism to social explosion. And this collective impotence continues to this day, a state of acquiescence, apathy and social torpor so profound that it seems at times that the paralyzed inhabitants of the Northeast are anesthetized. Poorly informed sociologists and anthropologists have attributed these psychological characteristics to the depressing and disintegrating effect of the tropical climate on the individual and collective will. Nothing could be further from the truth. The climate has nothing to do with such social behavior, which is conditioned exclusively by a way of life that never permitted the working people to organize as a *people*, and as such to win an active voice in public debate on the national destiny.

The feudal regime imposed by the planter class is also a key to understanding another social phenomenon so often misinterpreted: the mystics and bandit leaders who, until 1930, arose again and again to stride the somber stage of the *sertão*. As noted earlier, drought and famine are natural hazards in most of the backlands. This is unavoidable. But when the given hazards of the *sertão* environment are reinforced by a merciless social and economic system, the pain becomes intolerable. Ill-timed and sporadic local rebellions, such as those of Canudos, Joazeiro, Caldeirão and Pedra Bonita, are not merely incidental historical events, as many think; they are a very significant expression of the feudalistic mold of Brazil's colonial history. The banditry that from time to time terrorized the region, as well as the epidemics of mystic delirium and destructive hatred, were nothing but disordered and unco-ordinated expressions of a latent urge to revolt by a population fenced in like cattle in a pasture without grass. These outbursts of fanaticism and banditry represent aimless and desperate attempts to escape the misery of the Northeast. In a penetrating study Roger Bastide[10] emphasizes the fact that the messianic element in the typical backlands rebellion is in many cases only the expression of an enormous collective longing for a miraculous solution to frustrations that appear to them beyond political solution. The late journalist Rui Facó[11] analyzed the same phenomenon more fully and showed that these primitive explosions are generated in large part by the monopoly on land. "The situation of the rural poor at the end of the 19th century, and even right into the 20th, was no different than in 1856. It was more than natural, it was legitimate, that these people without land, possessions, rights, guarantees should seek an outlet in banditry and fanatic sects, in 'saints' and 'counselors,' as a means of realizing their dream of a better life."

The feudal agrarian structure also accounts for the social alienation, the total lack of conscience, typical of the elite of the Northeast practically up to our own day. Having risen to absolute power as if by mere fiat, and never having intermarried with the lower classes, this misbegotten oligarchy has lost its capacity to create; in effect, it has cut itself off from history. The great landowner's view of life is more ornamental than functional, and his culture and style of social behavior are full of blind and petty egotism.

To recapitulate, the people of the Northeast, to a notably greater degree than other Brazilians, suffer from cultural lag. They have been slow to develop into a social entity, and they have only limited and sporadic experience of common aspirations. The struggle for survival has left them little scope for social action. Meanwhile, battening down this dumbly suffering mass is a ruling establishment made up of people who are spiritually and socially abortive. These feudal mentalities do not identify with the peasants. Indeed, they take pride and satisfaction in being divorced from any responsibility for the commonweal. They believe themselves set apart as the few, made of different clay, born to rule and take and have, while the many serve them.

This dreadful impasse gives rise to great social pressures overlying and reinforcing the natural rigors of the backlands environment. But in every mass some people resist the general fate. This resistance often finds expression in religious fanaticism, visionary exaltation or violence for its own sake. However, there are signs of a dawning social and political consciousness.

This is the picture of the Northeast today, at the hour of its second discovery.

chapter 5

THE PEOPLE
OF THE NORTHEAST
AWAKEN

In the four centuries of agrarian feudalism—centuries of great suffering and very little progress—which followed the discovery of Brazil, the Northeast remained virtually stagnant. But when Brazil was "rediscovered" by the Americans in 1960, it was an entirely different story. This time the whole world was different. And most important, the Brazilian people had begun to find an identity.

In contrast to the discovery of Brazil, which occasioned no great stir, the "rediscovery" in 1960 had powerful repercussions. Dom Manuel, king of Portugal, kept discreetly silent about navigator Cabral's happy find. But the Americans used every means of communication to let the world know that they had found a deep pocket of unrest and social agitation right behind their line of continental defense.

The present inhabitants of the Northeast received the Americans in a way quite different from the original acceptance of the Portuguese. These second discoverers encountered suspicion of and even hostility toward their methods of dealing with backward peoples. To the Brazilians, this new trade relationship seemed little more than a sophisticated refinement of the bartering practiced during the first years of colonization. The Brazilians distrusted the Americans' paternalistic overtures of help and protection, and the press accounts of events in 1960 clearly reveal the atmosphere of suspicion and incomprehension.

Articles written by Tad Szulc for the October 31 and November 1 editions of *The New York Times* are typical. These pieces were read and commented on by President Eisenhower, and in this sense they played a role somewhat comparable to the letter in which Pero Vaz de Caminha announced the first discovery of Brazil to the king of Portugal. Szulc reported that a revolutionary situation was in the making in the Brazilian Northeast, brought about by the pressure of chronic impoverishment aggravated by periodic droughts. He further revealed that this misery was being exploited by a growing Communist movement in the overpopulated cities and that Communist infiltration of the Peasant Leagues had become an important political factor. The second article, "Marxists Organizing Peasants in Brazil," said Fidel Castro and Mao Tse-tung were being held up as heroes to peasants, workers and students. Szulc wrote:

"Recife is the support base for the southern string of tracking stations of the South Atlantic guided missile range of the United States Air Force. It services the stations at Fernando de Noronha, a Brazilian island off the coast here, and at Ascension Island, and is engaged in helping to set up the new stations off the African coast for testing new long-range missiles, including the Polaris. Support ships and cargo Globemasters are supplied in Recife, which also serves as a communications center for the southern section of the Cape Canaveral range. There is no noticeable anti-American feeling in Recife thus far. In World War II tens of thousands of United States servicemen were stationed here or went through Recife. But there is an undercurrent of resentment, based on the sentiment that after using the Northeast as a wartime base, the United States has done little to help it in peacetime."

Szulc turned next to the economic factor:

"There are sections of the arid Northeast where the annual income is about $50. About 75 per cent of the population is illiterate. The average daily intake is 1,664 calories. Life expectancy is 28 years for men and 32 for women. Half the population dies before the age of 30.

"The birth rate is 2.5 per cent annually. Gastric diseases take an enormous toll in babies less than one year old. In two villages in the state of Piauí, taken at random, not a single baby lived beyond one year.

"Tenant farmers working tiny parcels of land are often forced to labor three or four days a week without pay. The bulk of the Northeast residents are not consumers or producers in the economic sense. Physical survival is their only concern, and it becomes desperate when the periodic drought hits. While the misery in the Northeast has always existed in varying degrees, a series of new human, social, economic and political facts have arisen in recent years to turn this huge region into the scene of a potential revolutionary explosion."

According to Szulc, the situation was so bad that "the Northeast will go Communist and have a situation ten times worse than in Cuba if something is not done." He added that leaders of the Leagues were telling the peasants that their misery was unnecessary and urging them to fight for their rights.

"In Recife," he wrote, "the pressures are mounting. Out of a population of 800,000 about 400,000 are unemployed or just partially employed, and thousands more arrive daily from the rural areas. They live in 'mocambos'—caves and holes in the ground, or in shacks precariously perched atop stilts on fetid, low-tide marshes.

"When the tide recedes in the Jordão River, one of the three crisscrossing this city and flowing into the bay of the harbor, the dirty brown waters of the tidelands become suddenly alive with thousands of men, women and children, submerged up to their waists. They comb the bottom for *caranguejos*, the tiny crabs that are their main source of nourishment.

"They eat what they catch and sell the rest. Josué de Castro, a Brazilian nutrition expert from Recife who once was president of the Food and Agriculture Organization, called this the 'Cycle of the Caranguejo.' "

Toward the end of his article the *Times* reporter emphasized that "Nobody here, therefore, is surprised that Recife has long been the stronghold of Communism in Brazil."

The social tensions of the Northeast made a deep impression on Szulc, an experienced oberver, and his analysis of the socio-economic situation was just. But he made a mistake when he ascribed this explosiveness to the machinations of Fidel Castro and Mao Tse-tung and the example of the Cuban and Chinese revolutions. What was lacking in Szulc's attempt to decipher the enigma of the Northeast was a deeper awareness of the region's history and of the transformation of the Brazilian consciousness since the beginning of this century. During this past half century a sense of national identity has emerged, along with a growing awareness of the social realities of Brazil. Had Szulc looked more closely, he would have seen that the Northeast was becoming a tinderbox even before Mao Tse-tung's revolutionary victory in 1949, and certainly before the Cuban revolution in 1959. The fact is, the explosive tensions in the Northeast were guaranteed by the inherent defects of its social and economic system.

The independence of Brazil in 1822 put an end to the system of land grants and substituted a system of legal tenure. This was the first blow to the feudal land-ownership scheme, but it was quickly countered by an association between the planters and the wealthy bourgeoisie, which made possible the joint purchase of still more land and the continued establishment and maintenance of enormous latifundia. The so-called "Land Law" of 1850 was an attempt to curb these abuses, but in practice it threatened to make the big estates even larger and preserve them indefinitely.

The emancipation of Brazilian slaves on May 13, 1888, dealt another blow to the stubbornly resistant feudal structure, shaking even its foundations. But once again the latifundium survived. The slaveholding sugar planters, the class that had known days of splendor during the Second Kingdom, was ruined, but a new class arose to replace it— the *usineiros*, operators of large sugar mills. For after 1870 foreign capital came in to help establish modern mills throughout the Northeast, and these large mills had an insatiable appetite for land and cane.

This new class combined the functions of big landowner and entrepreneur. With their arrival, the production of sugar was revolutionized, but the archaic framework of the latifundium remained intact. While land monopoly was intensified in the Northeast, the situation in the South began to change. Free Europeans, who immigrated to Brazil on an average of 100,000 a year between emancipation and the end of the century, settled for the most part in São Paulo and made this state into the great coffee-producing center, shifting Brazil's economic axis completely and opening new social perspectives.

From then on, growing sugar cane fell into a more or less permanent slump, while the coffee growers became ever more prosperous; The national wealth of Brazil grew rapidly, and a bourgeois, capitalistic outlook developed. As capitalism penetrated into the countryside an embryonic rural working class appeared, and with the growth of the cities and the start of industrialization came the first signs of an industrial proletariat. The total effect of these changes was to generate a true Brazilian people, a self-conscious national entity responsive for the first time to all the demands and antagonisms of the various groups which composed it.

Under these pressures the latifundian system, previously a solid front united in concepts and objectives, for the first time was unable to avoid a split. The erstwhile lords of the land broke up into two groups: one remained impervious to progress and retreated into ultraconservatism and retrograde methods of production; the other saw the inevitability of evolutionary progress and opened their gates to the newer methods. The first group was recruited mainly from the great sugar plantations of the Northeast, while it was the South which embraced the new and vital posture. Thus two Brazils were created, the virtually feudalistic North and the capitalist South, both moving toward industrialization. With the proclamation of the republic toward the end of the last century, this dichotomy was accentuated. Once the nascent middle class of Southern Brazil entered the government, the sugar barons began to lose the political power they had exercised during the Empire.

The backwardness of the Northeast sugar economy aggravated the misery of the region, and social pressures were only slightly alleviated by mass emigration to other parts of the country. About the turn of the century thousands of peasants were drawn to Acre by the rubber boom and became part of that bitter page of history. After World War I they went to São Paulo, where the rapidly expanding industry and a prosperous agriculture absorbed more than 100,000 Northeasterners annually. Scattering into other parts of the country, broadening their narrow range of experience, the Northeasterners developed a better understanding of their own situation within the larger scene. They learned that at home they were pariahs, abandoned to social degradation. Chronic hunger and misery, which had seemed natural and inevitable to most of the peasants, like day and night, sleep and death, began to take on a different aspect; for now they knew that there were people in other regions to whom such hardships were unknown. Their lot was not decreed by Nature after all. It was not an act of God, from which there was no reprieve.

With new roads penetrating the Northeast and trucks appearing in the previously isolated desertland of the *sertão*, an idea of progress began to take vague shape in the collective consciousness. The people began to glimpse in material progress a force capable at last of emancipating them from their sufferings, something that neither independence nor the proclamation of the republic had accomplished, because both these events had failed to budge the ruling class and had excluded the people from their benefits.

When independence was won and the republic proclaimed, the people played practically no part in the drama. However, they learned a great deal from watching the main actors. And once they began to experience the impact of modern technology and its political and social consequences, they began to dream of mounting the stage themselves and competing for some of the more important roles in Brazilian history. Then, following World War I, when new means of communication brought a wider diffusion of ideas, the reality of the Northeast as different from the rest of Brazil took on greater clarity in the people's mind.

One factor highly influential in this process was an effort to democratize culture. It was begun in the capital of the Northeast and was carried out by young intellectuals who were tired of the kind of culture traditionally venerated in Brazil—arid and academic, divorced from social reality, derivative, designed for show rather than spiritual advance. This empty, passive, sterile drawing-room culture had always been useful as an antidemocratic tool for preserving the status quo. The archaic culture also helped to perpetuate the most painful expression of the country's backwardness—the enormous gap between the educated few and the illiterate many. Widespread illiteracy and ignorance have been deliberately perpetuated in order to hold together the feudal edifice, which threatened to topple under the least shock of new ideas. The ruling class of the Northeast has always lived in terror of ideas and of those who propagate them. For good reason they have resisted popular education and looked with suspicion upon bold spirits who dared to offer enlightenment. If the latifundium was to survive, not only vast tracts of land but the people as well had to be left unused and fallow.

But finally a breach was opened. In the 1920's a new form of literary expression appeared in Brazil—and by no coincidence, in the Northeast—a form of writing with popular appeal that was devoted to the problems of the people and the tragedy of their lives. Out of stagnation and fatalistic acceptance a sharp cry of protest suddenly rang out. From the midst of acquiescence arose a wave of writers in rebellion—the great novelists of the Northeast. They were called proletarian writers because they ferreted out the dark holes and hidden places known only to the poor. Around their writing was a strong odor of life, a smell nauseating to people who lived in cleaner places. The novels of Graciliano Ramos, Jorge Amado, José Lins do Rego and others heralded the self-discovery of the Northeast and laid bare its painful realities. They distilled and concentrated the diffuse sentiment of a people awakening to revolt against economic and social oppression.[1]

The same feeling of protest began to spread through popular poetry, a leaflet literature printed on cheap paper and sold at the backlands fairs. Out of fear of reprisal the country poet spoke in metaphors and parables, but with a wealth of poetic imagination. Few of the *sertanejos* are able to read, but the illiterate majority came to know this revolutionary poetry through the *violeiros*, the guitarists and singers who chant folk verse at fairs and festivals in the interior and transmit the rich body of Northeastern folklore from generation to generation. Many of these leaflets focused on topical problems such as land tenure and landlordism, and quite a few made eloquent contributions to Brazil's self-discovery. About two dozen small publishers scattered through the towns of Northeast Brazil are still printing and distributing this literature, and the peasants store it in the only kind of library they have—kerosene cans. Particularly notable among these folk writings is "The Arrival of Lampião in Hell." Lampião is the great *cangaceiro*, the bandit who has the whole back country in an uproar as he robs the rich to pay the poor and metes out his own brand of roughhanded justice. Speaking through a rifle barrel aimed at law and order, which he views as evils to be destroyed, Lampião is the embodiment of revolt. Contemplating the man and his exploits, we are reminded of what Sartre said in a letter to Camus: "For the present the human order is nothing but an unjust and precarious *dis*order, since in it people are killed and die of hunger."

The "hell" revealed by the peasant poet is like the house of the landlord, whom the poet visualizes as the Devil in flesh and blood guise. In this hell there is a fence, a gate, a watchman, a cotton storehouse—everything commonly found at the master's big house. The landlord symbolizes the satanic power against which Lampião, the peasant transformed into hero, struggles and comes out victor. The poet concludes with satisfaction:

> Great damage was done
> In hell that day;
> All the money was burned
> That Satan possessed.
> The record books were burned
> Plus six hundred contos
> In merchandise alone.*

But it is not only in literature that Brazil began to show clear signs of enlightenment. Before this, to escape reality, people either withdrew into solitude or fled abroad, but now, in all sectors of the national life, there were suddenly men who were profoundly interested in getting at the roots of their country's problems, in probing the basic causes and arriving at home-grown solutions. The men of this new Brazilian culture set out to combat the brutalizing effects of a way of life imposed by a small minority. With Portelo Eduardo they believed that "to be underdeveloped is to inhabit the periphery of the human condition, without ever having access to it." The prisoner of underdevelopment, as they saw it, *não vive, sobrevive*—"survives, but does not live." [2] This movement began to intensify about 1930.

* Houve grande prejuízo
No inferno, nêsse dia;
Queimou-se todo o dinheiro
Que Satanás possuía.
Queimou-se o 'livro do ponto'
E mais de seiscentos contos
Sòmente em mercadoria.

It was during this phase of Brazilian history that I became personally conscious of the realities of the Northeast region where I was born. I looked about me and saw, with youthful indignation, the spectacle of misery in the poorer sections of Recife. It was during this period that the oppressive images of *Geography of Hunger* crystallized; and about this time I also wrote "The Crab Cycle" (the commentary from which Tad Szulc quoted in *The New York Times*). I took a group of destitute people who were living in the mangrove swamps of Recife as a symbol of life in the Northeast.

> Things began to get tight. There was only one way out: to take to the swamps. No one pays rent in the mangrove swamps; you can eat crabs and go practically naked. The mangrove swamp is a paradise—not blue and rose with the tints of the celestial paradise, but black with the color of mud. A crab paradise.
>
> In the swamp the land belongs to no one. It belongs to the tide. When the tide comes in, it swells and stretches over all the land, but when it draws back it leaves the higher places bare. On one of them Zê Luis perched his shack. The walls were of mangrove stakes packed with mud, the roof of straw, dry grass and other materials from the dungheap. Everything free, found right there on the spot, in brutal comradeship with nature. The swamp is a real friend in need, it provides everything: room and board, shack and crabs.
>
> Now, when Zê Luis leaves for work in the morning, the rest of the family is already up and about. The boys jump from their bunks, out the door and into the swamp. They wash the sleep from their eyes with the muddy water, go to the toilet right there, and then jab their arms into

the mud for crabs. With arms and legs stuck in the mud, the Silva family has nothing to worry about. Zê Luis sets off for work content, because he is leaving his family deep in their own dinner, crawling in the mud that is crawling with crabs and crayfish.

The mangrove swamps of the Capiberibe are a mud-crab paradise. If the land was made for man, the swamp was made for crabs. Everything there is, was or soon will be crabbish, including the mud and the people who live in it. The mud is mixed with urine, excrement and other residues carried in by the tide, and whatever is not yet become crab, will be. The crab is born in mud and lives in it. It grows by eating from the mud, fattens on its filth and turns it into the white flesh of its claws and the greenish jelly of its viscera. On the other hand the people live there by catching crabs; they suck the claws, lick the shells till they are clean as a cup. And with this meat, made out of mud, they build the flesh of their bodies and the flesh of their children's bodies. They are a hundred thousand individuals, a hundred thousand citizens made of crabmeat. What their bodies throw off is returned to the mud, to be made into crabmeat again.

In their swampy backwash, unified and identified with the crab cycle, the Silva family has no problems. It has become one of the stages in this marvelous cycle. Each member of the family moves within this round of crabbish misery until the end, until the day of his death. When that day comes the pious neighbors will carry this mud, no longer alive now, to the cemetery of Santo Amaro, where it will proceed through additional worm and flower stages. Having accomplished these transformations, unknown in the swamp, the crab cycle seems to have been broken. But the relatives and descendants shed tears of mourning into the swamp, with them nourishing the mud that nourishes the crab, and the cycle goes on.

Such documentations of conditions in the Northeast led Brazilian scientists and politicians to seek a better understanding of the problem and a peaceful solution.

Brazil had lived for more than four centuries under a regime that upheld a colonial-type economy. But in 1930, with the revolution of Getúlio Vargas, the first clear impulses toward economic emancipation began to be felt, and they multiplied in popular manifestations of all sorts.[3] In step with their country's economic and technological development the people of Brazil were becoming increasingly aware of their social inequities; they wanted more and more to participate in the national political life. Industrialization had created an urban proletariat which had begun to have a voice in the distribution of power. But thanks to an organized patronage system, oligarchic groups calmly continued to manipulate their captive electorate up to 1930. Power was exercised by half a dozen front men who were handpicked by the elite and completely divorced from the collective interest. The electorate represented only a tiny fraction of the total Brazilian population, and elections were no more than a democratic façade. In every Presidential election prior to 1930 the number of votes cast never represented more than 3 per cent of the population.[4] An insignificant minority decided what the people should and should not have.

But in 1930 things began to change—not only because of the triumph of the Vargas revolution, mounted that year in Rio Grande do Sul (which actually, at bottom, was no more than a shift in power from one group to another, without any real mass participation). The more significant cause of the change was the depression of 1929. With Brazilian exports drastically reduced, there was no foreign exchange to buy foreign goods. This forced Brazil into makeshift "self-sufficiency," which naturally had a profound effect.

Since Vargas had completely identified with popular government, his election in 1950 as a "candidate opposing the Establishment" was the first electoral demonstration of an independent popular will. About 20 per cent of the population voted in 1950, and since then the percentage has been increasing. The theme of the political drama of contemporary Brazil is the awakening of great masses of people who previously had no economic power and no way of expressing their needs except by sporadic revolt. Today Brazilian political life is no longer a struggle between factions within a traditional ruling class, but between whole classes of people with profoundly divergent interests. It is the economic evolution of recent years that has given rise to this new polarization. Economic evolution has laid bare the basic problems and pushed Brazil to the crossroads.

On one side stands the Right, fighting desperately, through its use of economic power, to preserve a political overlordship in danger of slipping from its grasp. On the other side, still poorly organized, stands the Left, which lacks financial backing but has the advantage of being able to draw strength from the elemental energy of the masses. The Left is determined to rid Brazil of what it views as foreign intervention and exploitation. Between these two highly activist forces lies the soft democratic Center, which survives only by inertia, making concessions to the two extremes.

Without doubt, this most recent evidence of polarization was triggered by the fall of the Vargas government in 1954. Curiously enough, Brazilian historians and analysts tend to neglect this catalytic event in Brazil's political awakening. But from this point forward, after Vargas fell, Brazil's main political forces fissioned and polarized. The intensive opposition to Vargas was the first step in the campaign mounted by extreme reactionaries to set up a government based on force. The President's suicide and his accusing letter shocked the masses; it raised political debate in Brazil to a point where it embraced national economic problems for the first time and addressed itself to the whole tenor of national life. Now, finally, it became clear—as it never had before—that the Brazilian political dilemma was the result of a conflict of interest immanent in the very process of economic growth—in the steel and petroleum industries, for example—and that the fate of the country was dependent upon expanding foreign trade and securing better terms in international markets, as well as continuing the struggle to discipline foreign capital and control its clandestine intervention in Brazilian political life.[5]

Vargas' suicide aroused a collective anxiety among the people and thus enhanced Brazilian self-discovery. The nation's political consciousness matured abruptly, and public debate reached heights of intensity. It was a well-established practice to throw wool over the people's eyes by discussing economic and social issues in basically irrelevant moral terms. Now Leftists began to expose this device as a diversionary tactic, to denounce the use of irrelevant principles for the sake of gulling the masses. It became increasingly difficult for defenders of the status quo to dwell evasively on symptoms of underdevelopment instead of coming to grips with the causes. Nevertheless, a certain antidemocratic group, whose open sponsorship of a recent *coup d'état* provides a rallying point for the Right, continues to practice the familiar evasions.

Thus the shifting of the dynamic center of the Brazilian economy has had significant political effects. Under the pressure of new, and particularly industrial, interests, the ruling class began to lose its iron grip on the electorate, and the political bosses began to lose their *raison d'être.* The point was that if manufacturers were to sell industrial products within Brazil, the Brazilian masses had to be able to afford them. In some cases industrial progress gives rise to antagonism between capital and labor. But in Brazil this did not occur to any serious degree; instead, the clash was between the new industrial bourgeoisie and the residual feudalists. The latter still look to foreign markets, and regardless of national cost, defend whatever mechanisms ensure profit for the exporting sector of the economy. Ideologically, this divorces the feudalists not only from the Brazilian masses but also from the industrial bourgeoise.

The national political consciousness, which first took shape in the great industrial centers of the South, gradually began to crystallize in the Northeast as well. At first the main shock to the backward people of this region was the revelation of how poorly they lived in comparison with South Brazilians and many foreign peoples; for if Brazil as a whole is an underdeveloped country, the Northeast is the very nadir. The social distance separating the Northeast from the South is in some ways greater than the gap between advanced Western countries and some of their former colonies in Africa and Asia. The states of São Paulo in the South and Piauí in the Northeast, for instance, are as far apart economically as the United States and the Congo or Laos.

For some time, as I noted earlier, the general backwardness of the Northeast was attributed to unfavorable natural conditions and a poor racial composition of white, Negro and Indian. But sociological studies have discredited these climatic and racial theories. The situation could not be palmed off on the hot climate and miscegenation, but there was a remaining problem—drought. So now drought became the great villain of the Northeast.

This idea took such firm hold that the Northeast became officially identified as the Brazilian "drought area," a region almost completely godforsaken. The "flathead" of the Northeast was portrayed as a kind of Brazilian Wandering Jew or American Okie, an eternal migrant forever reaching out his scrawny hand to test for rain or to beg. The vested interests did their best to make periodic drought the scapegoat of the Northeast, but in reality not all of the Northeast is dry, and drought is by no means the basic cause of all calamity, even in the deep *sertão*. However, it took time to prove this and then to convince public opinion in other parts of the country that underdevelopment and starvation in the Northeast were mainly due to social and economic inequities, not to scanty rainfall.

In 1956, when the Northeast was in the grip of a major drought, I sought in a speech before the Federal Chamber of Deputies to show that the problem was complicated and that to save the Northeast merely by dealing with the effects of the dry spell would get us nowhere. Even at this late stage my sentiments evoked fierce opposition, including—what may seem stranger still—disclaimers from representatives of the Northeast itself. This discourse serves as another documentation of the progressive awakening of the Brazilian national consciousness:

I do not deny the existence of the drought. I deny that it is the cause of the phenomenon of hunger in the Northeast. The drought is a secondary, a subsidiary cause, which merely aggravates an existing state of affairs determined by other causes, that are social, rather than natural . . . I want to make my point of view very clear so as not to be misinterpreted, because as a Northeasterner, as a man of the drought region, as the son of a man of the *sertão* and as the grandson of a refugee from the 1877 drought, I do not deny the existence of the phenomenon. It is necessary, however, not to twist things by saying that the drought alone is to blame; the greater part of the blame lies elsewhere. My purpose is to clarify, and I have the courage to say that it is not drought that determines the (people's) starvation; there are other contributing causes that need to be removed, and I wish to suggest a plan to annul these causes, so as to put an end to the misery and hunger afflicting a large area of the nation. . . . In my view the famine in the Northeast . . . is a social rather than a natural phenomenon. More than drought it is generalized poverty that is responsible for this state of affairs, the progressive proletarianization of the *sertanejo,* his minimal and quite inadequate productivity, on account of which he is unable to accumulate any reserves to face the lean years, though with him there are no fat ones. Even when it rains his productivity is miserably small and his income minimal . . . And what are the causes of this social situation, this state of economic stagnation and progressive proletarianization in the *sertão?* In my view, the essential cause, the central cause we must all combat, is the inadequate agrarian structure of the region, the undesirable land tenure system, the existence of great estates side by side with tiny holdings that we find all over Northeast Brazil. Since this is essentially an agricultural region, with 75 per cent of the population living on the land and 50 per cent of income gained from agriculture, it can survive and develop only if agriculture is profitable and productive. Unfortunately this is not the case. And why is it not? Because the latifundium is the Siamese twin of technical obsolescence. The big estates pursue a primitive kind of agriculture, a proto-agriculture, without technical know-how, without fertilizers, without selective management, without mechanization. Everything is done in a most rudimentary way, draining the poor *sertanejo* in order to produce what turns out to be less than enough to satisfy his hunger.

The power of the latifundium in this region is indicated by the significant statistical fact that from 1940 to 1950, according to the demographic and agricultural census, the average size of agricultural holdings in the Northeast, far from diminishing, increased and is still increasing, so that today . . . only 20 per cent of the inhabitants or rural areas own land, 80 per cent work as renters, sharecroppers and colonists, all because the land is monopolized by a small group. To show you to what extremes this monopoly has gone, it is enough to mention the fact that 50 per cent of the total area of the Northeast is owned by only 3 per cent of all rural landowners.

On the other hand, more than 50 per cent of the properties contain more than 500 hectares [1,250 acres]. There are hundreds of properties with more than 10,000 hectares [25,000 acres] . . . Therefore it does not seem just to me that we should place so much emphasis on this drought phenomenon, because there are much worse things in the Northeast: the latifundial system and agrarian feudalism, for instance. Drought is a transitory phenomenon, but pauperism in the Northeast is there all the time. Transitory emergency measures against the drought, therefore, are not enough. What is needed are measures in depth, structural reforms that will really modify the economic framework of the Northeast region.

Today these ideas, which raised such objection at the time because they were felt to be heretical, are widely accepted.[6] Today everyone agrees—with the exception, needless to say, of the feudal oligarchy—that the evils of the Northeast derive from its traditional feudal economy. In the beginning the Northeast was a colony of Portugal. Later it became a colony of the South of Brazil—a colony of a colony, exploited by various power groups in colonial fashion.

chapter 6

THE NORTHEAST AND LATIN AMERICA

W<small>HEN</small> they awoke socially, the people of the Northeast became aware not only of their own regional problems but also of the fact that these problems related to the rest of South America. They realized that the difficulties of the Northeast are typical of Latin America, and that their economic geography could serve as model for the whole continent.

In order to demonstrate this truth—that the Brazilian Northeast is not an isolated problem, that it is typical of Latin American underdevelopment—this chapter will review socio-economic conditions throughout the continent. We would hope to arrive at a better idea of the region's position in the larger picture and at the same time help to gauge its relative explosive potential. Such a synthesis may also help correct the incorrect notion that there is no real anti-American sentiment in the area, as reported, for instance, by Tad Szulc in *The New York Times*, when he said that all he found was a certain resentment of the fact that the Northeast is not being aided in peacetime as much as during World War II.

In fact, there is strong anti-American feeling in the Northeast that arises from quite different and more serious causes. The Northeasterners harbor a confused animosity toward the United States which stems, among other things, from a lack of understanding of the American way of life. All the Northeasterner knows is the kind of treatment he gets from Americans doing business with and in Latin America. He sees these people buying cheap and selling dear. And he sees how the U.S. State Department backs them and allies itself with those Brazilians who are eager and willing to advance the exploitative process, provided they make a profit themselves. The Northeasterner fails to distinguish between the American people as a whole and, on the other side, that handful of Americans who actually do business with Latin America and that sector of the U.S. government which supports them.

Americans, of course, share in this mistake. If they think of the Northeast of Brazil at all, they are apt to consider it as a nest of dangerous Communist agitators. They assume that these agitators are stirring up a people who would otherwise be willing to wait patiently until a struggling Brazilian government righted their wrongs and overcame the defects of their environment. This notion is as woefully mistaken as the Northeasterner's of the United States.

Latin America is awakening to modern life and is wondering about its own possibilities; it is becoming conscious of its political and social obsolescence and of the paradoxes of an economic organization that places extreme misery and hunger side by side with almost insolent wealth. According to the Swiss economist Pierre Goetschin:[1] "After centuries of stratification and stagnation imposed by a strict feudal order inherited from the Iberian conquistadors and maintained by the complicity of the great landowners, the army and the clergy, the world of peasant and peon, of petit-bourgeois businessman and university intellectual is beginning to move in search of a different future. You may think what you like about Cuba, but there is no doubt that the revolution of Fidel Castro was a clear sign that the old order is degenerating and that there is a tremendous desire for change. This is the most notable fact about Latin America today."

"The social and economic structure of Latin America is decadent, corrupt, immoral and generally insolvent. It is obvious that a change is coming. That it will take the form of revolution is certain. That this revolution should imply the possibility of violence is inevitable. The question is: who will lead this revolution?" These are the words of the journalist John Gerassi,[2] who has lived in a number of South American countries. His grim prophecy has the ring of truth.

There is a great unrest throughout Latin America; a fierce search is under way for means of liberation from all forms of servitude.[3] This accounts for the self-criticism so typical of contemporary Latin American writing and for the objectivity with which modern Latin American sociologists and economists analyze the social and economic conditions on the continent. And it is also the reason they call for a complete revision of the concept of Pan-Americanism, to alter both the ideological and the political content. For Pan-Americanism can no longer satisfy the legitimate demands of peoples determined to rise and be free—to break the shackles of underdevelopment which have been imposed on them both at home and from abroad.

Latin America is an area of 9,000,000 square miles; it represents approximately 16 per cent of the world's inhabited territory, contains 220,000,000 people, about 7 per cent of the world's population. There are twenty sovereign states and a few colonial territories in this vast region which extends from the frontiers of the United States to the Antarctic Circle. Within Latin America there are immense reserves of petroleum and all kinds of minerals. Its potential is enormous in arable soils, which are still largely unexploited. Latin America is a much larger and potentially richer land mass than the United States, but its populations are extremely backward socially and economically. It has all the signs of an underdeveloped area: low average per capita income, a glaringly unequal distribution of wealth, high birth and death rates, widespread illiteracy, endemic diseases and general undernourishment. Annual per capita income is about $350, a third as high as in Western Europe, an eighth of the average in the United States. Differences in the levels of affluence are striking, not only between different regions of the same country, but between different social classes as well. Two thirds of the people do not have enough to eat; half suffer from infectious diseases and parasites; and more than half sign their names with a cross. At least a third lead a purely vegetative existence which is without economic or cultural meaning.

This state of imbalance is maintained by a feudal agrarian system. Latin American countries continue to depend mainly on extractive enterprises such as agriculture and mining. Most of their income is derived from exporting coffee, sugar, cocoa and tobacco, all produced under an archaic argicultural system. Meanwhile, as in other underdeveloped areas, the population grows rapidly. The rate of annual increase is the highest on earth—2.6 per cent, compared to .8 per cent in Europe and 1.8 per cent in the world as a whole. Since the annual increase in gross income in Latin America is not more than 4 per cent, only 1 per cent can be considered available for growth; the other 3 per cent is used up by the annual increase in population.

Where will Latin America turn, now that it is becoming aware both of its extraordinary potentialities and its alarming deficiencies? In the light of current conditions and ecocomic tendencies, almost no significant change can be anticipated in the foreseeable future. Only through a new effort, something different from the methods used until now, can the unrealized "continent of abundance" of the Iberian colonizer emancipate itself from its low estate. And for the time being, this herculean effort still lies in the realm of good intentions. "Private interest takes precedence over the public interest, and the foreign interest over the national interest. The twenty republics are permitted to enjoy political independence so long as they do not become so aggressive as to try to use it. Almost all of them depend on a single buyer-seller. They sell at low prices and buy at high ones. They depend on monopolies that proliferate like cancers. On a capitalist structure a feudal structure is superimposed . . . With a view to keeping and expanding their privileges, the feudal elements have granted foreign capitalism the right to cut the fruit at will, squeeze out the juice and impoverish these nations irremediably. This semicolonial situation awakens a bitter resentment, and prepares the scene for great political disorders." [4]

We used to think of Latin American history as an epic of discovery, a crusade to bring Christian light and faith to benighted heathen souls, to cultivate the spirit and nourish the body of primitive populations mired in ignorance and backwardness. The real history has been quite different—a long impoverishment and despoliation of the continent's natural resources by successive waves of colonial exploiters much more interested in salvaging the homeland economy than in saving the souls across the sea. The conquistadors were much handier with the sword than with the Cross. One sixteenth-century missionary, a true Christian, angrily demanded whether the great seigniors of his time carried the Cross of Christ or that of the thieves who hung at His side.

By the nineteenth century the colonial bourgeois revolution against the despotic mother country had run its course. But political independence did not lead to economic revolution. The inherent defects of colonialism remained untouched. For three centuries Latin America had been despoiled for the benefit of Spain and Portugal. When these two nations went into decline, Latin America continued in the role of a great supplier of raw materials and agricultural products, but now the United States, rather than Spain and Portugal, was the principal benefactor in the unequal trade relationship. While the Latin American colonies were winning their political independence, the United States bubbled with creative energy; it had extensive capital and technical resources that could be readily applied to the immensity of Latin America, where a docile labor force and inexhaustible natural wealth were to be found. The United States was strong, well armed, enterprising. It had the Monroe doctrine, which could be used, if convenient, as an excuse for intervening to preserve the status quo.

The people of the United States believed ardently in the virtues of liberalism and in their historic task of exporting efficient private enterprise while implanting democracy, and they threw themselves into this task with the same zeal that the Iberian peoples had shown when promoting the Christian faith. These new American pioneers believed that the advantages of an international division of labor were self-evident, an arrangement whereby some nations supplied raw materials and others, like themselves, refined and manufactured them. The result of this division of responsibility, they believed, was a general prosperity. And we must not underestimate the sincerity of their conviction. However, the actual effect of this system was to enhance economic imbalance and its dire social consequences.

In advancing this relationship, the United States assumed that Latin America would remain always acquiescent. The ruling class consisted of landed proprietors whose social and political importance was measured by the number of acres they owned and not by their ability to put them to use socially, as well as for private profit. Sharing their power were the businessmen and financiers, a class that revered the names of Montesquieu, Jean Jacques Rousseau and Auguste Comte. They loved the clichés of liberalism and were experts in drawing up constitutions decorated with eloquent declarations of the rights of man. But these constitutions, like so much else in Latin America, were only a democratic façade behind which the forces of inequity moved at will.

Even to this day Latin America suffers from a shortage of capital and has no pool of technical skills on which to draw. In general, the educational system still turns its back on the modern world. Instead of the epics of Morgan and Ford, the South American prefers the *Iliad* of Homer. For him classic poetry makes more interesting reading than profit-and-loss statements. Lacking the spirit of free enterprise, the drive to get practical things done, Latin America has expected the Western democracies to do what so far it cannot do itself. So it has committed its interests and its future into others' hands.

Western liberal capitalism left the rural feudalists in effect intact, while at the same time creating a well-heeled urban minority. As for the masses, they were either a lumpenproletariat in the towns or a debased peasantry on the land. In exchanging raw materials for manufactured goods, Latin America sold cheap and bought dear. Because of this the people have suffered and they still do. The results of the Latin American capitalist-feudalist hybrid economy have been deplorable. They stand out conspicuously for all who have eyes to see.

Venezuela sweats petroleum from every pore. Bolivia is plated with tin and Chile with copper. Brazil and Colombia transmogrify the humus of their soil and their people's sweat into coffee. In all directions American importers relieve Latin America of its raw materials, pile up the profits and leave nothing but misery behind.

Since 1945 Venezuela has been the world's second-largest producer of oil—185,000,000 tons of it in 1962. Thirty years ago it had 3,000,000 inhabitants, today it has 8,000,000. The oil workers do not live badly. They enjoy high wages as well as social, medical and cultural services, since petroleum supplies three fourths of the Venezuelan national income of $5,000,000,000 a year. The average per capita income is $800, high for South America. But arithmetical averages are grossly misleading. Oil workers are in fact only a tiny fraction of the whole population, and the great mass of people still live in the blackest misery. The $800-per-capita average actually comes from a purely imaginary distribution of multimillion-dollar incomes accruing to the very few.

Standard Oil produces half of Venezuela's black gold, Shell a fourth, Gulf a seventh, with Socony, Sinclair and Phillips accounting for the rest. These companies pay liberal taxes and royalties to Venezuela. But that did not keep the Standard Oil affiliate, Creole, from obtaining benefits calculated at $167,000,000 in 1950. These companies also own 15,000,000 acres of land as private concessions.

The second-greatest source of Venezuelan wealth, iron, belongs to Iron Mining. a subsidiary of U.S. Steel, and to Orinoco, a subsidiary of Bethlehem Steel. These companies are currently extracting 15,000,000 tons of ore for export. The Hawkin group has taken over petrochemicals, the Cooper group steelmaking. The lavish villas, the paved highways and the insolent skyscrapers of Caracas bear witness to the sparcely spread-out opulence, which is again only a façade masking the teeming misery of the slums. Four hundred thousand peasant familes cultivate land that does not belong to them, and the country today produces only half the corn, meat and milk that it consumes, and only a third of the vegetables and grain. As a result, according to Harvey O'Connor, "everything in Venezuela except raw materials costs 50–100 per cent more than in the United States." Even the minority of quite well paid Venezuelan workers cannot cope with the high cost of living.

In Peru, Anderson Clayton controls the cotton and wool. The Grace Company, Chase Manhattan Bank, First National City Bank of New York, Northern Peru Mines, Marconia Mines and Goodyear fix agricultural prices and control 80 per cent of the raw materials. A single Standard Oil affiliate controls 80 per cent of the national oil production. Two companies owning 32,000,000 acres of land reign supreme in the field of copper and other minerals. The monopolies enjoy considerable tax privileges. There is even a decree, dated October 11, 1945, classifying their profits and benefits as "strictly confidential information," and the repatriation of capital to the United States is shrouded in legalized secrecy. The current president, Belaúnde Terra, in order to avoid revolution, is seeking to carry out reforms, but he is up against the closed ranks of the economic oligarchy.

In Central America the United Fruit Company controls practically the whole economy of Guatemala, Nicaragua and much of Honduras. Railroads, port installations, ships, radio stations, newspapers—everything belongs to United Fruit. Meanwhile, its affiliates direct the importation of industrial products.

In Chile, Kennecott and Anaconda control practically all the copper mines and blast furnaces.

In Mexico all mining, as well as the nonferrous-metals industry, silver excepted, belongs to the American Smelting and Refining Company. Westinghouse dominates the electrical appliances market, Ford and General Motors the automobile industry, Pan American the airways and American Tobacco the manufacture of cigarettes.

It is the same story in other parts of Latin America. American monopolies control practically all economic operations. In 1959 the monopolies admitted having made a profit of $774,000,000 in Latin America. Indirect calculation shows that if the truth were known, the profit was closer to $1,250,000,000. According to the economist Johann Lorenz Schmidt, profits made in Latin America are 50 to 200 per cent greater than those made in the United States itself.

From 1920 to 1953 the American Foreign Company in Guatemala returned to its shareholders more than twelve times their investment. The Chilean economist Alberto Baltra has estimated that the American monopolies controlling the production of copper in his country have made a net profit of $2,000,000,000 in the last thirty years. This represents approximately 40 per cent of the total value of copper exported during the period and three times the size of the investment.

The loans granted to Latin America are widely publicized, but the conditions surrounding them are seldom discussed. The interest on the loans is moderate. But there is the damaging stipulation that the borrower must buy industrial goods in the United States.

In the wake of the great crash of 1929 various Latin American countries made an effort to create their own industries, and to bolster this project, they set up customs barriers. Unable to get their products through these barriers, the monopolies decided to install branch factories. They already controlled the extractive industries and much of the agriculture; now they took over most of the processing industries, usually giving them native names for window dressing. This sort of operation continues to this day. Consumers are often quite unaware that they are still paying tribute to an American trust. When Mexicans, for example, buy electrical wares from the Indústria Elétrica Mexicana, they are really swelling the profits of Westinghouse.

The countries of Latin America are also obliged to pay homage to the embargo on trade with Communist countries resulting from the cold war. When they have tried to sell certain raw materials to Communist countries they have been condemned as pro-Communist. President Janio Quadros of Brazil made tentative commercial deals with the Communist bloc, and at once his image in the American press began to decline; and it continued to deteriorate until his resignation. Since all the Latin American countries depend for their balance of payments on the sale of only one or two products, their economies are extremely vulnerable and can be controlled by foreign economic pressures, particularly by contrived fluctuations in the price of raw materials. A few figures will serve to illustrate how this kind of control can be applied. Some 74 per cent of Colombian exports consists of coffee; bananas account for 72 per cent of Guatemalan exports; copper accounts for 67 per cent of Chilean exports; tin for 62 per cent of Bolivian exports. Against this background, during the last ten years prices for typical Latin American exports declined as follows: wool, 46 per cent; zinc, 28 per cent; cotton, 23 per cent; tin, 20 per cent; cocoa, 52 per cent; coffee, 33 per cent. The prime complaint of the Latin American countries is that 75 per cent of all these exports go to the United States. One-crop agriculture and total dependence on one privileged buyer-supplier hogties the Latin American economy.

Becoming more deeply aware of this oppressive situation, the peoples of Latin America have grown to believe that if they merely follow a routine course of economic evolution, they will never break out of the iron circle in which they are trapped. Only through profound structural changes, changes which can hardly be brought about except through violence, will they ever be able to throw off their shackles. Today it is widely believed in the countries of the southern continent that neither international aid nor loans can prevent a continental explosion.

Against the general Latin American background the Northeast stands out as a small-scale model of the whole. Although industry has made inroads here and there, the economy remains fundamentally feudal and agrarian. Even the use of money as a means of exchange is still limited. Wage labor hardly exists, even on the largest properties. Working for a day's wages is most in evidence in the Pernambuco and Alagôas sugar belts but has hardly penetrated the other croplands of the region. Wage workers

number no more than 1,000,000 out of a population of 20,-
000,000, and by no means all of these 1,000,000 workers
receive wages free and clear as in genuinely capitalist
countries.

The greatest obstacle to uprooting the feudalism of the
Brazilian Northeast, as we have said again and again, is the
concentration of property in the hands of the few. At the top
of the social pyramid a tiny minority controls the lion's
share of the agricultural resources. Most people own nothing but the power of their labor. This amounts to so little
that the average Brazilian working man cannot even begin
to support his family properly. His earnings are perenni-
ally mortgaged. Debt hounds him all his life. The peasant is
denied not only economic but also educational opportunity,
which makes it extremely difficult, if not impossible, to
raise the regional level of income. The latifundian system
also suffers from a chronic shortage of capital. There is little margin for investment and a limited formation of surplus wealth. As a result expansion of agricultural enterprise or the creation of rural processing industries is virtually impossible.[5]

Because this defective land-tenure arrangement offers
no vital incentive to invest for greater and more efficient
production, the favored landowning few use their surpluses
in speculation or conspicuous consumption. Even government investment, of which there has been a considerable
amount in the Northeast, has failed to promote any fundamental change, since subsidy tends to flow through established channels. Let us see how it works.

Public dams are built to combat drought and increase
the agricultural potential of surrounding lands. Who bene-

fits from this? The big planter on whose lands the dam is built. The same thing happens with federally constructed irrigation canals. Meanwhile, the co-operatively financed dams and wells that are widely scattered through the region are usually out of the reach of all but the large and medium-sized proprietors. The small farmer cannot obtain technical and financial assistance from the government; he does not have financial resources of his own, and he has neither access to nor influence with the governmental authorities.

Many investment programs have been devised for the Northeast. But unless some means can be found of widening and varying the use of land, they are doomed to failure. The economic development of the Northeast and the success of official programs to combat drought depend completely on total agrarian reform. Agrarian reform based merely on the settlement of publicly owned lands is inadequate, an evasive stopgap, as are the proposals based on expropriation with indemnification at fair market value. What is really needed is total expropriation based solely on the public interest, a reform that would not only break up unproductive latifundia and give the land to those who need it for a decent life, but would also make for better rents, regulate labor contracts and fix adequate wage levels, and provide financial and technical assistance to small farmers. In short, a clean sweep is needed, a reform that would liquidate all vestiges of feudal privilege once and for all.

Anything short of these drastic measures, and the Northeast will continue slowly to decay and forever lag behind the rest of Brazil, its lethargic gait brought to a dead halt periodically by drought. Lacking this complete reform, the inequitable Northeast system of exporting raw materials and importing manufactured goods will continue unabated. The currently unfavorable balance of trade will tend to deteriorate still further, since international trade is extremely unfavorable to exporting raw materials in general and those of the Northeast in particular.

These are analytic, not merely impressionistic, conclusions, and they are supported by a careful reading of statistics. According to the Agricultural Census of 1950, only 49 per cent of the Northeast is used in raising crops. But this seems to be a gross underestimate. For if we discount urban areas, rivers, lakes and inaccessible mountainous regions, this would still leave a large acreage of empty public lands, and we know that such lands do not really exist. This error is due to the absence of rural land records. Owners are left to guess at the number of acres they own, and of course, they give a low figure to minimize their property taxes.

Out of the 125,000,000 acres described in 1950 as being agricultural holdings, only 10 per cent were actually being cultivated. This minimal percentage of employed land, added to the fact that 76 per cent of the farmers have less than 12.5 acres under cultivation, characterizes the latifundian structure. The data of the 1950 census may be suspect. But the census does provide at least a rough idea of the situation, which will become clearer when we examine the patterns of ownership.

First, we find that a large number of farmers in the Brazilian Northeast own no land at all. Out of a total of 4,697,000 people who worked on the land in 1950, only 749,000 were heads of farms, while 261,000 of these ran farms of less than 12.5 acres. This means that almost 4,000,000 Northeasterners were being forced to work someone else's land on a sharecrop, rental or wage-labor basis. Herein lies the main cause of the low productivity and investment rate. And even among those who do own land we find striking disparities. Some 15,458 large proprietors own tracts of 12,500 acres or more. That is, only 2 per cent of the rural population owns 48 per cent of the arable land. On the other hand, small owners, (those with less than 12.5 acres) represent 76 per cent of all owners but control only 14 per cent of the land. The drift toward pauperization is shown by a progressive increase in the number of very small properties. In 1940 the number of farms of less than 12.5 acres was 28 per cent of the total, but by 1950 this figure had risen to 35 per cent. So small are these holdings that the people who work them may be classed as a genuine rural proletariat. Meanwhile, the large properties remain intact; the rich get richer, and the poor get poorer.

These simple figures show how greatly land ownership in the Northeast of Brazil is concentrated. Contrary to the trend elsewhere in the country, both the degree of concentration and the average size of agricultural property increased in the 1940–50 period. Thus the monopoly on land is growing stronger, despite the tendency of Brazilian inheritance laws to dilute ownership. Figures on property of over 1250 acres confirm this fact. Property of this fairly large size is increasing both in the number of farms and in their average acreage.

Work relationships are also typically feudal. If capitalism has made some inroads in the sugar industry in the form of wage labor, in other agricultural sectors the customary setup is either renting or sharecropping, typical expressions of servility and exploitation. Whatever the relationship, the landowner always insists on short-term contracts, so that as his land increases in value he can renegotiate on more advantageous terms. The peasant who grows certain crops—cotton, for example—is badly used both by the landowner and the trust which processes and exports the product. Cotton is a considerably important factor in the backlands economy. But unlike growing and milling sugar, a self-sufficient operation, the growing and processing of cotton are separate functions. Cotton processing, together with the industries based on its by-products, is dominated by the powerful American firms of Anderson Clayton and Sambra. They own the mills, control commercial capital, monopolize the sale of agricultural machinery and buy all available raw material at their own price. Meanwhile, the business of raising the crop remains in the hands of the landowners. They own the soil but are vassals of the processors.

Stock raising in the Northeast operated for a long time on a share-and-share system: the cowhand kept one out of every four calves. This system prevailed while there was an open range and the natural pasture was a kind of collectively owned property. But as the value of beef rose and consumer demand increased, and as the herds improved in quality, it proved to the cattleman's advantage to pay the cowboy in cash, or to force him to sell his calf at whatever rock-bottom price the owner might stipulate.

It has also been the practice of landowners in the Northeast to expand plantings of agave, the sisal plant, for use as fiber in cordage and other products. The price for agave was relatively better than for other crops, and a large labor force was not needed to tend the plantings. When small properties could not supply enough sisal fiber for the hackling machines, not only temporary plantings, such as corn and beans, but also permanent crops were given up, to provide more land for the agave. New land was bought for this purpose and new latifundia appeared. The Brejo area in Paraíba—formerly divided into small, intensively cultivated farms which produced food for sale in the city of Campina Grande and also, during drought periods, to the population of Rio Grande do Norte, Ceará and Pernambuco—were seriously depleted by the sisal invasion.

The end result of this contempt for humanity and human resources is the fact that per capita income in the Northeast is only 38 per cent of the Brazilian average, and the illiteracy rate is 74 per cent, compared with a national average of 42 per cent. Another result is chronic unemployment, particularly in the sugar country. Here we see the "nomadism of the workers during the cane-cutting season, large groups coming down from the *sertão* and *agreste* to the cane belt, then returning each year, in a hopeless coming and going." [6]

Today the peasant of Northeast Brazil knows far more about the workings of this repressive system than one might suspect in an illiterate people. He understands that land monopoly, in league with a monopoly on exports, always tends to break the peasants' backs when prices are forced down by trusts. And it is his belief that the lords of the land, the middlemen and other accomplices in the patterns of exploitation, are the ones really responsible for holding back the region's economic development. He knows full well that they have robbed him of all purchasing power, down to his last penny; and he holds them to blame for his collective sufferings and hunger.

chapter 7

YEARS
OF DECISION

D<small>URING</small> that brief interval of "rediscovery" in 1960, when the American press and information services heavily publicized the Northeast, social tension there was already at the breaking point—a tension that had kept in step with the political awakening of the masses. The Northeast, as a typically backward area permanently engaged in a desperate struggle for social and economic emancipation, was experiencing something common to underdeveloped nations—a collective world-consciousness (or what Pierre Teilhard de Chardin has called a "spiritual tissue").

Despite forces which attempted by every possible means to prevent the formation of this collective consciousness and to restrict its attempts at expression, the endurance point was passed, and the barriers suddenly gave way.

The collective consciousness spilled out with such violence that in retrospect it seems not so much an evolutionary phenomenon as a kind of social transfiguration. For those who have not followed its incubation in the subsoil of a social struggle that has gone virtually unrecorded, there is something unpredictable and disconcerting about it all.

One of the foreigner's commonest impressions when he makes his first visit to the Brazilian Northeast is how certain rich personalities stand out against the formless conglomerate of the archaic and the modern. "Brazil collectively is an unpredictable world, a disconcerting world in certain respects, but one in which the mixture of races, the hostility and fecundity of nature, have engendered an exceptionally rich individuality. Expansive as a Southern Frenchman, melancholy as an Indian, tender and gentle as a Negro, the Brazilian asks himself why he should be so poor in a country that ought to be so rich. And so he is becoming conscious, that is to say, politically conscious." André Dumas made this observation after he had gone to study the Northeast of Brazil. He concluded that this country is a gigantic social force today, a potential not yet realized but approaching the time of release.

This creative force dammed up for centuries by feudalism is finally beginning to remake the social landscape, like waters about to rise in flood and sweep across the land, opening new channels as it goes. Meanwhile, successive governments attempt to anticipate the inevitable changes by initiating various programs. But most of these efforts have proved abortive; this is one more indication that complete political awakening, though on the way, is yet to be accomplished. So far the attempts to correct the Northeast's poverty and backwardness have been doomed from the start, thanks to conservative factions who are determined to uphold the status quo.

For centuries the major problem of the Northeast was thought to be drought, an uncontrollable climatic defect; and as a result, for a long time nothing at all was done to alleviate the people's suffering. It was only after the drought of 1877 had killed off half the population of the Northeast by hunger and thirst that the Brazilian central government took action. Even so, it provided only an emergency relief program for the victims and did not attempt to attack the underlying causes of the disaster.[1] One would not realize this, of course, from the misleading official title of the first "National Commission for the Study of the Problem of Drought." For years this commission, in a sporadic and aimless way, dispensed relief during emergencies. Finally, in 1909, in response to constant complaints about the commission's ineffectiveness, another agency was created which was charged with drawing up and putting into effect a plan for combatting drought. The new agency was called the "Federal Inspectorate of Works Against Drought."

The creation of this agency was strongly motivated by that blind faith of the early 1900's that science and technology can provide solutions for every problem. But this blind faith had a practical example in the Bureau of Reclamation, set up by the United States in 1902, and successful initiation of a large-scale irrigation program in the arid Southwest.[2] Thus inspired, the inspectorate became a kind of engineering agency. Arrojado Lisboa was named the first director and stayed on for three years. Since he assumed

[160]

that the water shortage was the basic problem, his entire approach to rehabilitation rested on a search for ways to provide and conserve water. Being so limited in outlook, the new agency was a failure from the start. Its main achievement was to build some dams and back up streams into great lakes. But the lakes were never used for irrigation. They merely served to reflect the blue of the hot Brazilian sky and to provide refuge for *retirantes* in times of drought. The same agency was also responsible for distributing aid to drought victims. But most of these funds ended up in the pockets of the landlords and their hangers-on, who squandered resources that should have gone to feed, educate and generally uplift the peasants. In brief, the agency became a nest of political corruption.

In the years 1919–22 the Drought Inspectorate was lavishly financed because for the first time in Brazilian history a man from the Northeast, Epitácio Pessoa, was President. Large sums were appropriated for public works, but again the move was negated by the narrow technological orientation and administrative corruption. Then, with the election of a President from Central Brazil, the *mineiro* (from the state of Minas Gerais) Artur Bernardes, almost all inspectorate funds were cut off. Works under construction were dropped in the middle. Expensive machinery bought from the United States by the previous administration was left to rust in the fields, alongside the sun-whitened skeletons of cattle dead from thirst. Once again the people's hopes were frustrated. In 1950 the inspectorate became a department, but politics continued as usual. The department remained alienated from the real interests of the Northeast. But if the new department was ineffectual in promoting better use of land, at least it made a series of surveys and studies that gradually revealed the social and economic realities of the Northeast. The department's scientific and technical contributions thus played a key role in forming the regional consciousness and envisaging more realistic solutions.[3]

Beginning with the Vargas administration, it became clearer that a new approach was needed. During the great 1931–32 drought the federal government provided relief for 220,000 victims through public works. These appropriations—10 per cent of the federal income—were the largest amount of tax money spent on the Northeast since the days of Epitácio Pessoa, when the figure had been 15 per cent. Nevertheless, under Vargas results continued to be inconclusive, and the problem unresolved.

The realization that distress in the Northeast was a problem not only of engineering and public works but also of economic reform led to the creation of two new agencies. The São Francisco Valley Company, a kind of Brazilian TVA, was set up in 1948 to use the river for producing hydroelectric power. The Development Bank of the Northeast was established in 1952. From this time on, a "development mentality" took root, in open opposition to the earlier policy of paternalism, which had created a welfare pork barrel for political parasites.

During the 1950's the Brazilian economy surged upward, and the average annual rate of growth reached 7 per cent, one of the highest in the West. During this period industrial production increased on an average of 10 per cent a year. With the industrialization of the Brazilian economy proceeding at this accelerated rate, the democratic consciousness of the country was proportionately strengthened and the masses began to feel a correspondingly greater desire for active participation in the affairs and destiny of the nation. These developments tended to bring down the obsolescent feudal structure, to threaten ancient interests and at the same time to provoke a violent reaction. And it is in the Northeast that the forces of old and new clash most directly. Everything in the region has begun to have ideological connotation. Everything is Right or Left, reaction or revolution.

A whole complex of converging socio-economic factors has determined this crystallization of attitudes into the sharpest and clearest alignments ever known in the Northeast. What the sociologist W. Ogburn calls a "cultural lag" has widened; traditional gaps and breaches in the social structure have increased to the verge of rupture.

President Juscelino Kubitschek, elected in 1955, was deeply committed to the ideology of development. He concentrated all federal effort on national development and emancipation. But he confided this task to people who were deeply compromised by their connections with the feudal agrarian faction and foreign capital. As a result, the deployment of effort was lopsided, limited mainly to industrial South Brazil. The intensive industrialization, since it concentrated on the South, threw regional imbalance still farther askew. Enlarging the regional imbalance between South and Northeast and the functional imbalance between industry and agriculture only served to aggravate the basic problem of hunger and a lack of even minimal social security in the deprived region. Ulterior motives were at work here, ensuring preferential treatment for the South and further enrichment of already powerful elements. Farming in the Northeast—which is basically an agricultural region— continued to be marginal because of feudalist insistence that agrarian patterns remain untouched. Let the government make all the industrial revolutions it wanted, but the slightest reform in land use was taboo. This left the Northeast hobbling about on one leg, hopelessly out of the running in any race toward industrial growth. By concentrating all the federal attention and resources in the South and Central part of the country, in effect by sacrificing everything to a new Moloch, the Kubitschek administration threw the national economy out of whack. Faced with a choice between bread and steel, the government put all its eggs into the industrial basket, forgetting agriculture completely and thus ending up with an industry starved for raw materials. Kubitschek's intentions were good. His goal was industrial independence for Brazil. But his plan fell short. Agrarian obsolescence put a check on industrial growth, and in the years following 1955 the rate of industrial growth began to decline: the yearly increase in gross national product dropped from 11 per cent in 1950–54 to about 5 per cent.[4]

Another factor aggravating social tension in the Northeast has been the increasing pressure from a growing population. The Northeast has a high birth rate, which leads to forced migration—and the frequent movement invalidates statistics on population. From 1950–60 population in the Northeast grew only 2.8 per cent annually, as against 3.6 per cent in Brazil as a whole, one of the highest rates in the world. But the great pressure of population in the Northeast is revealed in the large-scale migration of its inhabitants to any corner of the country where there is a chance, real or illusory, for a better life. The Amazon region at the beginning of the century and São Paulo in more recent years have absorbed this unemployed surplus of manpower.

With the failure of the rubber boom in the Amazon region and the relative recession of industry in São Paulo, population pressure in the Northeast had to increase. Brasília was built during this period; but its demand for labor, large as it was, could not absorb the surplus of unemployed. The Northeast is threatening to saturate Brazil with its driven masses, exporting its misery far and wide. And everywhere the Northeasterner goes, he takes with him his anguish and spirit of revolt and nonconformity. André Dumas has aptly noted that if New York has its proletariat of Puerto Ricans and Harlem Negroes and Paris has its rootless Algerian immigrants, then in Brazil today a Northeastern proletariat is ubiquitous. Every Brazilian city, from Pôrto Alegre in the extreme South to Brasília in the center, has its Northeasterner, camped beside the luxurious urban buildings, an exhibit of human trash scattered by hunger's lash and drought's burning winds.

The Northeast is clearly the No. 1 national problem in Brazil. The scattered presence of Northeasterners reinforces ideological struggle and provides new arguments for opposing groups. The Right and the Left, or confused forces that presume to be such, are clashing aggressively in the national political arena. The principal characteristic of the Brazilian Left is that it takes a democratic political position while advocating economic revolution. It believes that the play of democratic forces will eventually bring populist pressure groups to power. Its tactic is to seek a legislature—under Goulart for a brief interval the traditional bicameral legislature became a "parliament"—that will be an authentic expression of all the people's needs. It looks to an executive capable of advancing measures supported by the popular will. It propagandizes vigorously against American and other foreign economic intrusion. The Left also seeks to win support among the armed forces, which today are sharply divided. The overwhelming majority of the military are patriotic and nationalist, but a small minority are so blinded by their anti-Communist obsession as to be quite capable of any extreme, however oppressive, in defending the status quo.

Against the infiltration of the Left, which is obviously gaining ground and even threatening to seize control through the ballot box, especially if the vote should be extended to the awakened masses, the Right violently rebels. The conservative Right wants above all to preserve the present national structure, thus ensuring its economic as well as political power. The Brazilian Right by no means represents a class in eclipse, dreaming of a return to power. Rather it is a politically active faction with a central position in the power structure, and it is determined to keep this position, even by subversive and undemocratic means. So it is that the Right—extremely conservative economically—is in the political sense revolutionary. These people see a genuinely democratic order as the greatest danger to their privileges. It would be the end of their world if the Left, already so potent at the ballot box, should actually take over the driver's seat.

There is virtually no centrist political position in Brazil. A true middle class has never existed in this feudal kind of society; a middle-of-the-road point of view has simply never developed to any extent. Those with centrist leanings try to adjust in a timid and ineffectual way to pressures from the two extremes.

Rightist ideology accepts total submission to foreign interests under the worn-out pretext of resisting the Communist menace. It exaggerates this "menace" to enormous proportions, meanwhile concealing the reality—the Brazilian Communist Party has never been strong and currently is badly split by the ideological struggle between Soviet Russia and Red China.

In its superficial analysis of the problem of underdevelopment in the Northeast, the Right defends the false thesis that national poverty is due above all to the lack of people capable of leadership. Some of its spokesmen place great emphasis on defective education and public health, which they see as causes and not effects of underdevelopment. The whole Right without exception refuses to face up to the built-in defects of Brazilian society. In view of such an interpretation it is easy to understand why the Right should have no democratic program to offer as a corrective to the backwardness and poverty. Violence is the only resort the Right knows—how to intimidate its opponents. This impulse toward terrorism produces a climate of anxiety and even panic throughout the land.

The Brazilian Right knows that its last and only chance lies in civil war, and if this developed, it could count on substantial foreign aid under the pretext of combating the threat of Communist dictatorship. But it is clear that civil war would be a dubious solution, in the long run doomed to failure. It can only be hoped that whatever solutions are undertaken to relieve the poverty in the Northeast and the general imbalance of the Brazilian economy will be democratic in nature and will not be sidetracked by Rightist adventures. Much will depend here on whether the United States refuses to be sucked into the situation on spurious anti-Communist grounds.

The complex Brazilian political scene is filled with paradoxes that are easily misinterpreted. The biggest error made recently by foreign observers was to minimize the extent of Brazilian unrest (which is total) and make it appear that certain personalities and political groups were causing all the disturbance. This was putting the cart before the horse: the real protagonist was the people, above all the amorphous and long-suffering masses of the Northeast.

Miguel Arrais, Francisco Julião and the Peasant Leagues, the priests of the agrarian-reform movement, Celso Furtado and the technicians of the SUDENE (Superintendency for the Development of the Northeast) have all been accused of agitating for social revolution in the Northeast. But these people and movements merely represent a variety of forces which are all going in the same general direction—toward emancipation. It is naïve to suppose that Julião invented the agrarian problem in the Northeast, that Arrais created the desire to be freed from peonage, that Celso Furtado made the Northeast economy what it is, or that I invented hunger.

None of us invented anything. The problems, desires and movements sprang spontaneously from the social structure of the region and were charged emotionally by a climate of despair. But to no avail. Through ignorance or bad faith, effects are persistently viewed as causes. To refute this erroneous interpretation—which, by promoting further suppression, can only augment the danger of a violent explosion in the Northeast and possibly set off a chain reaction through all of Latin America—we need only objectively analyze what has been happening in the critical years since the "rediscovery" of Brazil in 1960. Who are the leaders seeking remedies in the Northeast? And what methods do they propose?

Two of these people are Miguel Arrais, the mayor of Recife in 1960, and Pelópidas Silveira, then vice-governor of the state. Tad Szulc described them as follows in his articles for *The New York Times:* "Recife's mayor, Miguel Arrais de Alencar, is generally described as a Communist, though he disclaims it. The city administration includes several known Communists in high positions . . . The state's vice-governor, Pelópidas Silveira, belongs to the Brazilian Socialist Party, which, in Pernambuco, works closely with the Communists, especially in the Peasant Leagues."

But is Miguel Arrais really a Communist? Indeed he is not. He is a practical politician with a relatively limited cultural background and no imagination. In general he is a pragmatic sort of person who wants to get things done. As a politician Arrais has devoted himself sincerely to the problems of the people and to a search for democratic solutions. During his administration as mayor of Recife and later as governor of the state, he surrounded himself with a team of technical advisors, among whom, it is true, there were Communists. But the group also included Socialists, devout or nominal Catholics, and simple economists and technicians, many of whom had a horror of ideological embroilment.

They all worked together to achieve a common goal—the socio-economic transformation of the key state of the Northeast, Pernambuco.

In an article published by Antônio Callado[5] in the conservative *Jornal do Brasil* in December, 1963, we read the following:

"At this moment Pernambuco is the greatest laboratory of social experiment and the greatest idea factory in Brazil. It is the most democratic state in the Federation. There you notice at once that democracy is not the usual type found in Brazil. Two main factors have combined to favor the appearance of this Pernambucan climate of freedom: a movement of mass agitation which in a few years has provided the masses involved with an education they never had before, and the election, as governor of the state, of a man of the people. Miguel Arrais is the first man of the people to govern one of the most backward yet at the same time most aristocratically pretentious regions of Brazil.

"Two things make it difficult to form any definitive opinion in Pernambuco about what is happening and what is going to happen: everything there is new, fluid, accelerated and, in the second place, everything is empirical. The social question in Pernambuco was, in the rigorous concept of the old Republic, 'a case for the police.' And it was the police, indeed, who solved the case. This is clearly seen in the memorandum that the Pernambuco entrepreneur class delivered in October to the President of the Republic and to the presidents of the Chamber of Deputies, the Senate and the Supreme Court, denouncing the 'climate of terror and insecurity' created by the Arrais government. The communiqué said: 'Within the same technique . . . the police

often participate passively in these invasions. The police
stand to one side, allowing events to unfold at will. In this
way they serve the government's purposes, and build up a
feeling in the peasant, who formerly respected law and authority, that he can follow the agitators without risk into
[paths of] disorder and crime, without fear of the police
force, which they themselves used to consider the guarantor
of public order.'

". . . The Pernambucan police, actually, are behaving
as policemen should, enforcing the law, that is, without being an instrument of repression. They do not go to work
with their nightsticks when the millowner calls, and this
creates a longing for the good old days among people who
used to count on the police as a docile watchdog. Participate
passively. Be a detached witness. And last November this
impassive police force guaranteed perfect order throughout
a general strike that completely paralyzed the whole Pernambucan sugar industry for two days. There were no attempts to damage or steal property, no deaths or depreda-
tions of any sort. Any carnival in Rio de Janeiro results in
many more accidents and disturbances than this bid for
more wages by 200,000 men who, until recently, scarcely
knew what wages were, let alone demands for pay increases.

"Everything is new and everything is empirical. Pernambuco is not like Cuba, not like the USSR. On the other
hand, it is no longer very much like the rest of Brazil. Its
poverty continues to be enormous, but its revolutionary activity, a search for solutions in all fields, gives it a vitality
greater than most any other state's. Democratic freedom is
complete. The major newspapers and the sophisticated lo-

cal television stations are conservative, the contraband traffic in whiskey and American cigarettes is cheerfully unconcealed. But at the same time there you have priests who see nothing to get excited about in the work the Communists are carrying out among the farmers, there you have the Peasant Leagues preaching guerrilla warfare in the name of Father Cícero of Joazeiro, and there you have a new generation working for nothing at union headquarters."

This article clearly reveals that Miguel Arrais is in tune with a historical movement. He trimmed his sails to the way the wind was blowing instead of making a grab for power.

As for Pelópidas Silveira, he has always been above all a progressive administrator, not a social agitator. He was always a good boss, one who never beat his workers or had them arrested, who respected them as men and considered them his brothers. It was for these reasons that the Recife proletariat elected him mayor twice. His supposed extremism is based exclusively on his stubborn refusal to cooperate with the blindly anti-Communist forces of reaction.

But there is still Julião—Julião the Antichrist, Pharisee, ogre, and his reckless Peasant Leagues. Julião himself has boldly laid his cards on the table: "We wish to make it very clear that having begun, some years ago, a work of agitation in the Pernambuco countryside, which later spread to the rest of the country and even outside our borders, the only title we wish to achieve at the end of this journey, if we deserve it, is that of a simple social agitator, in the patriotic sense of someone who brings a fundamental problem before the people so that it may be frankly debated and a just solution found." [6]

The problem that so deeply disturbed this man was the agrarian feudalism of the Northeast, with all its attendant poverty and social injustice.

Who taught Julião how to "agitate"? He learned by himself, in the rugged school of the Northeast. Julião was a self-made leader of the people. All about him he felt the latent resentment of age-old abuse, responded to it and spoke out. The spectacle of oppression was more than he could stomach and he rose up against it. It was much the same with Julião as centuries before with Frei Bartolomeu de las Casas, who protested against his fellow Spaniards' mistreatment and slaughter of the Indians. And similarly, Joaquim Nabuco, compelled by a deep sense of outrage, campaigned for the abolition of Brazilian slavery. And for Antônio Silvino and Lampião the decision was banditry rather than submission to the back country landowners.

As it always happens when a folk hero emerges to champion the people against their oppressors, Julião was condemned by the establishment as a rabble rouser. But it must be realized that long before the advent of Julião the Northeast was becoming aware of the root evils of the lati-fundian system: the payment of ground rent, or *foro*, and the tradition of exacting free or cheap labor, or corvée. In 1961 the Brazilian journalist Mauritonio Meira wrote: "In truth the peasant is a prisoner of exacted labor and ground rent, institutions which are the chains of feudal servitude. To use the land the peasant must pay the owner an annual ground rent, or *foro*, of somewhere between 10 and 40 thousand cruzeiros. Beyond this he is subject to the corvée . . . system, whereby he must contribute 99 days of work a year, 90 of them (in the various cases we have examined) at a daily wage of 4–5 cruzeiros, and the 9 remaining days for nothing. During the corvée the peasant receives no food ration, not even a glass of water, for which reason it is called a 'dry corvée.' In case the peasant, because of sickness or some other reason, cannot contribute the required number of work-days, he is penalized by having to pay for each day lost at the going rate for the same kind of work on a non-corvée basis. This means that for work that would bring him 5 cruzeiros he must forfeit 80–100. Besides the payment of ground rent and forced labor it is also common for the landowner to demand that the peasant work certain areas of the land even though it may be extremely difficult and unremunerative for him to do so. As with the corvée, if the peasant cannot work on the '*conta*,' as the expression goes, he must pay someone else to do it for him at the going wage. And there are still further aggravations. The *foreiro*, or sharecropper, must sell what he raises to the landowner, and at whatever price the owner wishes to pay. Even then payment may not be in cash, but in supplies or cane spirits. The foregoing system is common on plantations in part given over to the growing of sugar cane, in part rented out to sharecroppers. Where the plantation-sugar mill uses all the land, the system is even worse. The cane fields begin at the peasant's back door. All day long he is in the fields, hoeing, planting, cutting, tying, loading the cane. Here the company store setup rules the scene. Staples are provided through the store in exchange for work at wages dictated by the owner. Little if any money ever changes hands. Now and then some mill owners try to dupe the worker into thinking he is making more than at other mills. Wages are increased, but the difference is immediately recouped by raising prices at the company store."

In the middle of the nineteenth century the whole Northeast was dominated by a handful of families. At one time a single family owned and operated practically the entire state of Pernambuco. As one writer notes:[7] "The three Cavalcanti brothers dominated Pernambuco: the Visconde de Camaragibe, the Visconde de Suassuna and the Visconde de Albuquerque. The first was the head of the Conservative Party, the second belonged to the Conservatives and the third was the unopposed leader of the Liberal Party. Changes in imperial policy had no repercussions in Pernambuco. The Cavalcantis were untouchable. This, it is said, moved Jerônimo Vilela de Castro Tavares, a law professor of Olinda, to write the following verse:

> Prepare for certain disenchantment,
> If you should live in Pernambuco
> For all but Cavalcantis there
> May not ride, but must be ridden.*

"This oligarchy represented domination by the rural aristocracy, a class which controlled agricultural life and owned innumerable big estates in the Province."

A century later the same old oligarchy was still riding the sad, old nag of the Northeast. The Cavalcanti dynasty

---

* Quem vive em Pernambuco
Deve estar desenganado.
Ou há de ser Cavalcânti
Oh há de ser cavalgado.

(Note the play on words: "Cavalcanti," a name of Italian origin, means rider, postilion; and "cavalgado" in Portuguese means ridden.)

might have passed, but the Ribeiros and the Lundgrens had swung into the saddle. As Antônio Callado wrote in 1963: "Paraíba is a state within the latifundium of the Ribeiros. Or so they say in Paraíba. Whatever the Ribeiros don't own of Paraíba belongs to the Lundgrens. Oh yes, senhor! The Ribeiros have all the flatlands of the Paraíba do Norte River, complete with all cities, towns and cane fields, not to mention the conscience of Paraíba's representatives in the National Congress. In addition to a big piece of Paraíba, the Lundgrens own the coast of Pernambuco and the Rio Grande do Norte, also a powder factory and the 'Casas Pernambucanos' chain stores. In these backward dukedoms of the Northeast grow cane and cotton cultivated by sharecroppers and day-laborers. But weeds also grow there, too, in the form of the Peasant Leagues."

Where such woefully depressed conditions are prevalent, even facing up to the subject at all cannot help but give rise to agitation. The lightest touch shakes a mass so rotten. Julião actually began his campaign against oppression by coining a simple but colorful language easily understood by the masses, though within any other context it would have been only mildly inflammatory, if inflammatory at all. He liked to say things like this:

"No happiness is possible on an empty stomach."

"Hunger cannot be put off or put away: either you kill hunger, or it kills you."

"We must put an end to this swindler society."

"We are not interested in anybody's religion or ideology: let's just get together, everybody, and free the peasant from oppression."

[176]

"We don't view the soldier, the priest, the student, the industrialist, the communist as an enemy; the enemy is the big landowner."

"The League will take the policeman away from the worker's door."

"So far only the League has brought the big landowner into court."

"The League is like a clenched fist. To hold the knife, we need such a fist. Let us unite like one."

"This struggle is nobler than the abolition of slavery."

"Either we will get agrarian reform, or agrarian reform will beget revolution."

"We will put through agrarian reform either by law or by struggle."

"Pope John XXIII was the first Pope of peasant origin. His recent encyclical is proof that the Pope supports the Peasant Leagues."

"The League is like a river in flood: it begins small, then grows and carries everything before it."

"In our preaching we use the words of the Bible. Yes, because the Bible is a revolutionary book."

With such mild apothegms of diverse ideological connotations Julião strove (as he described it) to channel into one river all the emotional wellsprings of the Northeastern *caboclo*—"hillbilly," the Americans would say—all his anguished resentment of social injustice, his urge to revolt against abusive minority privilege, his religious feelings and his capacity for aggression in hours of decision. Julião made a tenacious effort to free the peasant from his muteness, by talking to him and teaching him to talk. And the peasant learned to think and use his tongue. The resulting interchange between peasant and his master is illustrated typically in the folk story below:

"Senhor Colonel," the peasant says, "what is this Communism anyway?"

"Communism?" the Colonel replies, very sure of himself. "Why, Communism is a government that takes away everything that belongs to other people, that mistreats people's daughters and attacks their religion."

But the peasant is even more sure of himself. "If that's the way it is, Senhor," he says, "we've got it here right now."

What dangers lie in this open dialogue between the now awakened masses and their ancient masters? One observer[8] has this comment: "The danger is not in Julião as such, the man who reads Jules Verne on the sly, but in the masses whom he is bemusing and egging on. Responsible elements among the Northeast intelligentsia are convinced that, in point of fact, Julião has served to hold back armed revolution in the region. For these intellectuals it is a lucky thing that the situation is still in the hands of Julião, who makes the Bible his primer like a latter-day Francis of Assisi. Catastrophe will come, however, if the sorcerer is unable to control the angry waters he is conjuring up. It is even possible that Julião may be carried into violence by the very masses he is now inciting. He may even be crushed by them."

Actually, Julião was not crushed, but left behind. The wave rolled ahead and over him. Other charismatic figures now ride the crest. It was not that he lacked capacity for leadership. He failed because of his inability to work out a

clear plan of practical action. In the end his verbal magic
dissolved into the mists of political romanticism. But the
energies which he released generated other leaders.

Now the Church has moved into the picture. The priests
were well aware of the people's misery. They also knew full
well into what low esteem the Church had fallen among the
masses. Galvanized by Julião's successes, they began to organize a social-action movement of their own with the more
progressive Catholic leaders in charge. The Church re-
solved to use the people's religiosity as a creative social
force. "The religious sentiment of these people is very
great, but, since the Church is held in such low regard, it
was useless . . . because it was as unchanneled as the
Drought Department's dams, which failed to flow into the
irrigation ditches. The *caboclo*'s religious feelings were
held back. God had become an unused wellspring of good
in the peasant nature. And anyone who could release these
living waters, no matter for what purpose, would have the
power at his command of a river in flood." [9]

Thus the Church, or at any rate some factions within it,
moved to intervene in the Northeast's drama of liberation.
Although the Brazilian Catholic Church has all the trappings of power, its religious content is relatively small. The
Church's power over the people derives mainly from the
fact that Brazilians are naturally averse to both religious
fanaticism and anticlericalism. The people believe without
question that the faith of Jesus Christ is man's salvation.
Brazilian Catholicism may have more form than substance,
but the masses still find nourishment in the Christian example. Even such typically Brazilian folk ceremonies as the
macumba and the *candomblé* of the Northeast backlands

[179]

and the slums of Rio de Janeiro interweave (in dance and song) Christian themes and African sexual and fetishistic themes. The basic motivation for these ceremonies is a hunger for divinity.

Like all contemporary Brazilian institutions, the Brazilian Church is deeply divided. Most of the hierarchy are politically conservative, indifferent to social problems and therefore an important contributor to the forces of oppression. But there is an enlightened minority, the so-called Catholic Left, centered mainly in the Northeast. The attitude of this wing, which is led by a majority of the bishops of the Nordeste, is reflected in a comment by the present Archbishop of Recife, Dom Helder Camâra, to the effect that "the scandal of it is not Communist infiltration, but the lack of Christian infiltration."

In recent years a number of priests have tried to organize farmers' unions in competition with the Peasant Leagues started by Julião. This departure from the policy of never forming peasant associations for fear of having the Communists take them over shows that at least some of the clerical element are deeply concerned. Forced to make a choice, they are now willing to risk unions as a lesser evil than revolution. One of the outstanding figures in this Church-led struggle against the latifundian system is Monsignor Negreiros, a priest from Seridó, a sugar-plantation area in the Northeast back country. Monsignor Negreiros answered his critics by saying: "If they keep on calling me a Communist, I'll buy a red scarf and wear it around my neck." Negreiros has warned the landowners that they can no longer count on the uncritical support of the Church. Of the landowners this Seridó priest has said: "They limit themselves to giving alms to the Church, and I am against this mere lip service to Christian principle. Christian charity without social justice is a poisonous thing."

Another famous priest in the Northeast is Father Melo, who joined forces with Julião from time to time and sided with the peasants against Cid Sampião, governor of Pernambuco, when he ordered them expelled from certain areas in the state. Full of fear, some of the farmers told Father Melo that they really had to leave because otherwise the police would come and beat them up, but the priest replied: "Don't worry. I'll excommunicate the police if they start that business." Father Melo holds to the theory that justice for the peasant does not involve ideological commitments. All he has to do is demand rights already guaranteed and carry on with his duties. "The agrarian revolution," he told Mauritonio Meira, "has to be carried out neither peacefully, as the capitalists say, nor violently, as the Communists say. Historical circumstance itself will prescribe the form of the revolution. If results cannot be gained peaceably, then we shall have to face up to the reality of outright struggle. But this does not necessarily mean total political commitment one way or the other." He continues his explanation with a metaphor: "When we start down the road in a car, we cannot tell in advance what gear we are going to use everywhere along the way. The road itself governs the choice of gear, and the road cannot be entirely prefigured. So it is with agrarian reform." [10]

When Catholic priests begin to think like this, it is obvious that the situation has reached a point of no return. One commentator[11] has written: "The clergy of the Northeast is the most advanced in Brazil, which as everyone knows is the largest Catholic country in the world. And the new clergy of the Northeast is the most advanced in the region . . . They are sons of the Northeast themselves, accustomed since childhood to its problems . . . This explains how easy it is . . . to find priests, monsignors and even bishops who seem revolutionary in the way they talk and act . . . Their approach is based not only on Biblical teachings . . . but above all on the latest papal encyclicals, such as the 'Rerum Novarum' and the extremely plain-spoken 'Mater et Magistra.' A reporter in the Northeast can easily find 'radical' opinions among the clergy of Petrolina, Garanhuns, Natal, São Luís and Sergipe . . . This is because these people are actually at grips with real problems. They are inside the situation, working through word and deed for an immense legion of the damned."

Meanwhile, in such a tense social climate small intermittent explosions are inevitable. In 1956 a group of peasants in the town of Goiana, in Pernambuco, fired on police who were trying to break up their League, causing several casualties. In a similar incident, also in Pernambuco, five peasants were killed. Both times the "police" were deputies hired by the landowners, which is permissible under Brazilian law.

From time to time too the drought intervenes in the continuing give-and-take of the struggle. In 1958 one of the worst dry spells in Brazilian history challenged the Kubitschek administration. Up to this point Kubitschek had virtually forgotten the existence of the Northeast in his preoccupation with the building of Brasília and the crash industrialization program in the South. Now the government was forced to divert a large part of national credits to the

Northeast to save millions of drought refugees from starvation. The Drought Department alone had to find employment for 500,000 peasants. Much of this money went into the pockets of "industrialists" of the drought—professional parasites who live off federal welfare programs. A national scandal loomed, and Kubitschek sent a member of his military staff to the Northeast to find out just what was going on. He was greeted by chaos and administrative impotence. Barring emergency measures, the prospects were either revolution or a separation of the Northeast from the rest of Brazil, or both. This crisis led Kubitschek to set up in 1959 the Superintendency for the Development of the Northeast, or SUDENE, as it soon became known. SUDENE was shortly to be bitterly criticized as a nest of social and economic agitation.

For the first time a really comprehensive and objectively planned reorganization of the regional economy was undertaken. Up to this point, the Northeast had never had the necessary political power to initiate federal assistance for regional economic development. Decisions on federal aid had always been made by men from other parts of the country; and markets of the Northeast had always been controlled either by foreigners or by businessmen from Rio Grande, Rio de Janeiro and Minas Gerais, who cared nothing about the people's plight. The final result of centuries of neglect was a trauma of the spirit in the Northeast, a bankruptcy of leadership. SUDENE now undertook to remedy this unhappy situation.

The task force was headed by the economist Celso Furtado. His first report revealed the total failure of federal policy in dealing with the Northeast. However, because some of his closest collaborators overemphasized technicalities, Furtado was misled at first and did not fully comprehend the entire web of inimical forces which were containing and impeding regional progress. In this first report, "A Policy of Economic Development for the Northeast," he attributed much of the poverty of the region to "the poverty of its physical base, the soil" and put forward a systematic industrialization of the Northeast as the solution to its problems. The feudal agrarian social structure was not even mentioned, as though it did not exist.

Presently, however, when he gained more first-hand experience as superintendent of SUDENE, he began to see the situation in its totality and to pay attention not only to industrialization but to the much more serious and immediate agricultural problems. Very soon the SUDENE technicians discovered they were helpless before legal barriers carefully erected through many years to serve the entrenched minority of landowners. And now, like the Catholic hierarchy and priests of the Northeast, these men of science were driven into the camp of agrarian reform, thereby increasing the pressure for a new deal for the peasants of the backlands.

This general development, and the much more pressing threat posed by the Castro government in Cuba, led President Kennedy to set up the Alliance for Progress as a counterrevolutionary instrument, though the full extent of this objective was never plainly stated at the Punta del Este conference in 1961. The American plan was presented to the Latin American countries, and U. S. Secretary of the Treasury Douglas Dillon announced that his country was prepared to lend decisive aid in furthering the economic

revolution of the whole southern continent. A month earlier, however, in sending a message to Congress requesting
funds, President Kennedy spoke of a "special military program intended to guarantee the internal security of Latin
America against subversion." [12] *The New York Times* reported that the new program represented a complete change
in the structure of military programs for the Western Hemisphere since 1952. The main objective now was not to
equip and train men for a joint defense of the hemisphere
against outside attack, but to insure internal defense against
subversion. In spite of these conflicting themes of economic
aid and defense against internal revolution, a real tremor
of hope swept the Punta del Este conference.

What did the United States propose to do through the
Alliance for Progress? The general drift was to assist Latin
America through $20,000,000,000 of loans and private in-
vestments over a ten-year period. In return, the Latin
American countries were to undertake profound fiscal and
agrarian reforms. But how did the promise work out? Upon
close examination it appeared that a great deal of the $20,-
000,000,000 was actually to come from private investors
and from aid and credits given by European countries, Ja-
pan and international banking institutions. The basic
American commitment was to be $1,100,000,000 a year, or
$11,000,000,000 over ten years. There was some question
among Latin Americans as to how the United States government was going to secure the remaining $9,000,000 from
foreign powers and international bodies, but this was allowed to pass.

When it came to actually applying the promised credits, the United States government proved dilatory and was

only too willing to distort the avowed aims of economic progress.[13] The role of the Alliance in the Brazilian Northeast is a good example. The entire Northeast, with its 25,-000,000 impoverished inhabitants, has so far received only one half as much aid as the state of Guanabara, with only 4,000,000. People in the Northeast say this paradox has arisen because the governor of Guanabara is partial to American interests, whereas the governors of the Northeastern states are responsible only to the people of their region.

To date no substantial agrarian reforms have been forced, by way of counterconcession, from Latin American governments, including the government of Brazil. The only form of appeasement so far has been "colonization" programs. Meanwhile, 2 per cent of the agricultural proprietors continue to monopolize 60 per cent of the land, and the latifundium reigns on. Invariably the United States backs down when the rich and powerful object. The United States will cling to any faction in Latin America, including the feudal oligarchy that is dead set against economic and political reform, under the colossal misapprehension that it is somehow defending the West against Communism. Discussing this in *The Great Fear*, John Gerassi says: "Today the oligarchies control most of the armies, police forces, banks, congresses and, in general, the state machinery. And those who denounced this control—smeared as Fascists not long ago—are branded Communists by Latin America's press as well as our own. Corruption is common in every Latin American country. Courts never convict the rich. Union leaders who complain of wage and living conditions are 'traitors,' while those who make deals with management

and government are the so-called democrats or Free Union-
ists."

What remains today of the splendid bark, launched at
Punta del Este, its sails bellied out with winds of hope?
Nothing but nostalgia and regret. In the years that followed, the United States continued its normal rhythm of aid
and investment, while private capital began to avoid Latin
America. In 1962 alone foreign capital was repatriated to
the tune of $18,000,000 more than new investment.

For obvious reasons the Alliance for Progress is a thor-
oughly unpopular institution in South America, and nowhere less so than in the Brazilian Northeast. More enlightened people understand how difficult it is for the United
States to pick and choose among partners or allies in the
continuing struggle against international Communism. But
they are also keenly aware that every time the United States
embraces a Latin American oligarchy merely because it
gives lip service to anti-Communism, this only enhances in
the long run the danger of revolution and a Communist take-
over. And they also realize that it is not easy for the United
States to co-operate with progressive elements that are truly
dedicated to democracy, because most of these people are
anti-American.

However, despite the difficulties, the choice is clear.
The anti-Americanism of the democratic groups is far from
meaning that these people dislike Americans as such. Their
disaffection does not apply to the American people, but to
traditional American policy, which is seen in democratic
quarters as invariably conducive to reaction and social injustice. And until Washington's attitude toward the Latin

American problem, of which the Brazilian Northeast is typical, undergoes a great sea change, no amount of aid and advice will be able to suppress the emergence of the masses.

This is the dramatic situation in the Brazilian Northeast, a situation symbolic of the whole southern continent on which the United States should meditate. Today, when isolationism means national suicide, when solidarity among nations is necessary, the countries of the Western Hemisphere cannot live in ignorance of each other, divided by a complete lack of understanding. If the countries of the Western Hemisphere really wish to defend and reinforce democracy, they must realize that defending democracy involves something other than preserving abstract principles and existing systems of advantage. It is the plight of the people that must engage their closest attention, the masses who are denied in order for a few to enjoy great wealth and freedom, a freedom too often construed as license.

In the Northeast, or even Brazil as a whole, every proposition—all the aid from the Alliance for Progress and all the plans for international co-operation to engender balanced economic growth—is irremediably doomed to fail unless it is accompanied by basic domestic reforms. Lacking this reform—the first of which must be to abolish the feudal agrarian system—the Alliance, instead of helping the Brazilian people, will actually help their enemies. The end result of these inadequate efforts of relief would be to foment revolution.

It must be appreciated that the explosive situation in the Northeast, the same situation that exists in different degrees of intensity throughout all Latin America, is not a product of Communism. Rather it is the product of the feudal oligarchy, of a class of people who make a career out of using Communism as a smoke screen. And in the Alliance for Progress these reactionaries smell a good chance to line their pockets, strengthen their political bases and perhaps reduce the rebellious people of Brazil to permanent servitude.

The suicide of Getúlio Vargas, the resignation of President Jânio Quadros and the crushing pressure applied on the government of President João Goulart when he sought to carry out reforms are clear indications of the power of the backward Brazilian "Establishment." And always, to repeat beyond any doubt or misunderstanding, the members of "the Establishment" fall back on the false claim that they are defending Christian civilization and democracy against the dangers of Communism, as if it were Christian and democratic to starve people for the sake of maintaining an oligarchic system of privilege.

As the current social tension grows, the forces of reaction feel increasingly imperiled and excuse ever more frequent violence and suppression on the grounds that Communism must be contained. It is quite possible that in this last-ditch defense they will actually trigger a total social explosion in the Northeast. This explosion may occur on the Right or on the Left. In either case, democracy may well blow up with it and be lost.

This is the lesson that both North and South America may learn from the Brazilian Northeast.

Source Notes

SOURCE NOTES

Introduction

1. Vaz de Caminha, Pero, *Carta a El-Rei D. Manuel,* 1500.
2. Ferrarote, Franco, *La Sociologia come Partecipazione,* 1961.

Chapter 1

1. Prado, Jr., Caio, *História Econômica do Brasil,* 1945.
2. Sánchez Albornoz, Claudio, *La Edad Media y la Empresa de América,* 1934.
3. Keyserling, Hermann, *Journal de voyage d'un philosophe,* 1952.
4. Cascudo, Luiz da Câmara, *Viajando pelo Sertao,* n.d.
5. Julião, Francisco, *Que são as Ligas Camponesas,* 1962.
6. Hirschmann, Alfred, *Journey Toward Progress,* 1963.

Chapter 2

1. Mello Noto, João Cabral de, *Cemitérios Pernambucanos,* 1952.
2. Vaz de Caminha, Pero, *Carta a El-Rei D. Manuel,* 1500.
3. Harlow, Vincent T., *A History of the Barbados, 1625–1685,* 1926.
4. Lippman, Edmund O. von, *História do Açúcar,* transl. by Rodolfo Coutinho, 1932.
5. Ragats, L. J., *The Fall of the Planter Class in the British Caribbean,* 1928.
6. Shepard, Ward, *Food or Famine—The Challenge of Erosion,* 1945.

7. Picard, François, *Les Phénomènes sociaux chez les animaux*, 1933.

8. Rocha Pita, *História da América Portuguêsa*, n.d.

9. Simonsen, Roberto, *História Econômica do Brasil*, 1937.

10. Quintana, Epaminondas, "El Problema Dietético del Caribe," in *América Indígena*, Vol. 2, No. 11, April 1942.

11. Teixeira, A. da Silva, "Contribuição ao Estudo do Solo de Pernambuco," in *Arquivos do Instituto de Pesquisas Agronômicas de Pernambuco*, No. 1, March 1938.

12. Freise, Friedrich, "The Drought Region of Northeastern Brazil," in *Geographic Review*, July 1938.

13. Mota, Mauro, *Paisagem das Sêcas*, 1958.

14. Gauthier, E. F., *Le Sahara*, 1928.

15. Luerzzelburg, Philipp von, "Estudo Botânico do Nordeste," in *Boletim da I.F.O.C.S.*, No. 57; also see Loefgren, A., "Notas Botânicas," in *Boletim da I.F.O.C.S.*, No. 2, 1923.

16. Cunha, Euclides da, *Os Sertões*, 1904.

17. Abreu, Capistrano de, *Capítulos da História Colonial*, n.d; also see Sodré, Nelson Werneck, *Formação da Sociedade Brasileira e o Oeste*, n.d, and Simonsen, Roberto, *História Econômica do Brasil*, 1937.

18. Prado, Paulo, *Retrato do Brasil*, 1928.

19. Zollinger, J. P., *À la conquête de la Californie*, 1939.

20. Loefgren, A., "Notas Botânicas," in *Boletim da I.F.O.C.S.*, No. 2, 1923.

21. Castro, Josué de, and Pecknick, Emilia, "Valor Nutritivo de la Mescla del Maiz con la Leche," in *Archivos Venezolanos de Nutrición*, Vol. II, No. 2, 1951.

22. MacCollum and Simmonds, *The Newer Knowledge of Nutrition*, 1929.

23. Rocca, Juan, and Llamas, Roberto, "Estúdio del Frijol como Alimento," in *Archives of the Institute of Biology of Mexico*, n.d.

24. Neves, Carlos Alves das, "A Batateira Doce e sua Cultura no Sertão e nas Bacias de Irrigação dos Açudes do Nordeste," in *Boletim da I.F.O.C.S.*, Vol. XVI, No. 2, 1941.

25. Von Spix and von Martius, *Através da Bahia*, transl. and with notes by Pirajá da Silva and Paulo Wolf, 1938.

26. Marion, *Las Maravillas de la Vegetación*, 1873.

27. Almeida, José Américo de, *A Paraíba e seus Problemas*, 1937.

28. Guerra, Felipe, *Sêca contra a Sêca*, n.d.

29. Nascimento, Nicanor Nunes do, and Vieira, Bernardo, *Vernos*, n.d.

30. Morel, Edmar, *Padre Cícero*, 1946.

31. Pinheiro, Aurélio, *À Margem da Amazônia*, 1937.

32. Almeida, José Américo de, *A Bagaceira*, 1936.

33. Barroso, Gustavo, *Heróis e Bandidos*, 1917.

34. Pereira, Père Joaquim José, quoted by J. Américo de Almeida in *A Paraíba e seus Problemas*, 1937.

35. Sorokin, Pitirim, *Man and Society in Calamity*, 1942.

36. Almeida, José Américo de, *A Bagaceira*, 1936.

37. Spengler, Oswald, *El Hombre y la Tecnica*, 1921.

38. Ortega y Gasset, *Dos Prólogos—a un Tratado de Montería, a una História de la Filosofía*, 1944.

39. Nansen, F., *Farthest North*, 1897; also see Peary, R., *Northward over the Great Ice*, 1898, and Mikelsen, E., *Lost in the Arctic*, 1913.

40. Ernst Kretschmer, *Théorie et pratique de psychologie médicale*, 1927.

41. Oliveira, Xavier de, *Beatos e Cangaceiros*, 1920.

42. Barroso, Gustavo, *Heróis e Bandidos*, 1917.

43. Arinos, Afonso, in Preface to *Terra de Homens*, by Ademar Vidal, 1944.

44. Bastide, Roger, "O Messianismo e a Fome," in *O Drama*

Universal da Fome, 1958, and *Brasil, Terre de Contrastes,* n.d.

45. Gruschmann, F., *Hungersnote in Mittelalter,* quoted by P. Sorokin in *Man and Society in Calamity,* 1942.
46. Albornoz, Sánchez Claudio, *La Edad Media y la Empresa de América,* 1934.
47. Figueiredo, Fidelino de, *Últimas Aventuras,* 1943.

Chapter 3

1. Lery, Jean de, *Viagem a Terra do Brasil,* 1941 edition.
2. Merea, Paulo, *História da Colonizacão Portuguesa,* Vol. III, 1947.
3. Azevedo, J. Lucio de, *Épocas de Portugal Econômico,* 1947.
4. Albornoz, Sánchez Claudio, *La Edad Media y la Empresa de América,* 1934.
5. Parkinson, C. Northcote, *East and West,* 1963.
6. Lima, Oliveira, *Pernambuco e seu Desenvolvimento Histórico,* 1895.
7. Caminha, A. Passos, *Quatro Séculos de Latifúndio,* 1963.
8. Simonsen, Roberto, *História Econômica do Brasil,* 1937.
9. Antonil, A. J., *Cultura e Opulência do Brasil por suas Drogas e Minas,* 1923 edition.
10. Koster, Henry, *Travels in Brazil,* 1817.

Chapter 4

1. Fleiuss, Max, *História Administrativa do Brasil,* n.d.
2. Dussen, Adner van den, *Relatório sôbre as Capitanias Conquistadas no Brasil pelos Holandezes,* 1639.
3. *Ibid.*
4. Brito, Rodrigues de, *A Economia Brasileira no Alvorecer do Século XIX,* n.d.
5. Freire, Felisberto, *História Territorial do Brasil,* 1906.

6. Lima, R. Cirne, *Terras Devolutas*, n.d.

7. Vasconcellos, J. M. P., *Livro das Terras*, 1860.

8. Prado, Jr., Caio, *Formação do Brasil Contemporâneo*, 1953.

9. Myrdal, Gunnar, *Une Economie internationale*, 1958.

10. Bastide, Roger, "O Messianismo e a Fome," in *O Drama Universal da Fome*, 1963.

11. Facó, Ruy, *Cangaceiros e Fanáticos*, 1963.

Chapter 5

1. Castro, Josué de, *Documentário do Nordeste*, 1935.

2. Portela, Eduardo, *Literatura e Realidade Social*, 1963.

3. Quintas, Amaro, "Vocação Política e Tendências Ideológicas do Nordeste," in *Síntese Política, Econômica, Social*, No. 17, January 1963.

4. Ramos, Guerreiro, *A Crise do Poder no Brasil*, 1961.

5. Mendes, Candido, *Nacionalismo e Desenvolvimento*, 1961.

6. Barros, Souza, *O Nordeste*, 1957.

Chapter 6

1. Goetschin, Pierre, "Situation economique de l'Amérique Latine," in *Revue economique et sociale*, February 1962.

2. Gerassi, John, *The Great Fear*, 1963.

3. Hanke, Lewis, *Colonisation et conscience chrétienne au XVIe siècle*, 1948.

4. Sweezy, P. M., and Huberban, L., *Latin America?* 1963.

5. Barreto, Leda, *Julião, Nordeste, Revolução*, 1963.

6. Moraes, Manoel H. A., "O Nordeste, o Meio e o Homem," in *Síntese Política, Econômica, Social*, No. 17, 1963.

Chapter 7

1. Teófilo, Rodolfo, *História da Sêca do Ceará*, 1922.

2. Hirschmann, A. O., *Journey Toward Progress*, 1963.

3. Pompeo Sobrinho, T., *História das Sêcas*, 1958.
4. Castro, Josué de, *Le Dilemme Brésilien: Pain ou Acier*, 1963.
5. Callado, Antônio, "Revolução Pilôto em Pernambuco," in *Jornal do Brasil*, December 29, 1963.
6. Julião, Francisco, *Que são as Ligas Camponesas?* 1962.
7. Meira, Mauritonio, "Nordeste, as Sementes da Subversão," in *O Cruzeiro*, November 11, 1961.
8. *Ibid.*
9. Callado, Antônio, "Revolução Pilôto em Pernambuco," in *Jornal do Brasil*, December 29, 1963.
10. Meira, Mauritonio, "Nordeste, a Revolução de Cristo," in *O Cruzeiro*, December 2, 1961.
11. *Ibid.*
12. *The New York Times*, July 4, 1961.
13. Lleras Camargo, A., "The Alliance for Progress," in *Foreign Affairs*, October 1963.

Index

Josué de Castro, a native of the Northeast of Brazil, was born in Recife, Pernambuco. He is a physician, an expert in nutrition, and has taught at the University of Brazil. In 1945 Dr. Castro was appointed head of the Institute of Nutrition at the University of Brazil. The author also served as chairman of the United Nations Food and Agriculture Organization. He was elected to the Brazilian Parliament in 1958, and since that time served as Parliamentary observer of the Brazilian government at the United Nations and, in 1963, as Brazil's ambassador delegate to specialized agencies of the United Nations in Geneva.

Since the military coup in 1964, Dr. Castro has lived outside his country. He is, at present, the President of the Centre International pour le Développement in Paris.

Josué de Castro is the author of the classic *Geography of Hunger*, which was published in the United States in 1952 and has been translated into eight languages. In addition, his other books and articles have appeared in editions in Europe and South America. He edited, with Irving Louis Horowitz and John Gerassi, *Latin American Radicalism: A Documentary Report on Left and Nationalist Movements* (available in Vintage Books).

VINTAGE POLITICAL SCIENCE
AND SOCIAL CRITICISM

A free catalogue of VINTAGE BOOKS *will be sent at your request. Write to* Vintage Books, 457 Madison Avenue, New York, New York 10022.